POLITICAL
HEAT

POLITICAL HEAT

John Nieman

Copyright © 2021 by John Nieman.

Library of Congress Control Number: 2021917462

HARDBACK: 978-1-955955-73-7
PAPERBACK: 978-1-955955-72-0
EBOOK: 978-1-955955-74-4

All rights reserved. No part of this publication may be reproduced, distributed, or transmitted in any form or by any electronic or mechanical means, without the prior written permission of the publisher, except in the case of brief quotations embodied in critical reviews and certain other noncommercial uses permitted by copyright law.

Ordering Information:

For orders and inquiries, please contact:
1-888-404-1388
www.goldtouchpress.com
book.orders@goldtouchpress.com

Printed in the United States of America

Dedication

For my good friend Jim

CONTENTS

1

The advantages of being mayor

Politics can be an aphrodisiac, as Graham Kruse had discovered through 20 years of public service.

As the mayor of New York City, he learned that people hung on his every word, and automatically assumed he must be smarter than some of the sentences that occasionally came out of mouth. They also supposed that he must be more popular, worldly and agile than anyone else around him. Otherwise, how could have been elected to the top office in America's biggest city?

Of course, he had plenty of help in shaping his positive image. Like most politicians, he had a rather educated and sophisticated staff that protected him from missteps. Consequently, the risk was low and the respect level was high, given his elevated position.

Kruse had a loyal cadre of professional men and woman around him through most hours of the day (and sometimes the night). Some of the men had been with him more than a decade. For the most part, they were lawyers, police and fire chiefs, deputy mayors, and a rather substantial group of accounting and financial visionaries.

The women that surrounded him were speechwriters, public relations professionals, school board pros, and administrative staff. The mayor often enjoyed visiting with them, since they tended to have a better sense of humor than many of the men. Graham often found himself smiling and even laughing around these women.

Besides, they were prettier than the men…and that often made his day, even though he tried his best not to flirt. However, it was often a losing battle, since Graham was "touchy/feely" kind of public servant. He often liked to link and handshake with a hug, And with women, he tended to couple it with a kiss on the cheek.

Even in the early years of his courtship and marriage to Linda, she had noticed this tendency, but tended to write it off as the behavior of super friendly guy. Even when they were in college at Princeton, she observed that he would often put his arm around his girlfriends, and even her girlfriends. Somehow, she believed that bringing this up to Graham would potentially cause a ruckus. He would ask "Has anyone complained?" At the time, she would have to say no. And so, she lived with it.

After he graduated from law school, and she got her master's degree in education, they moved in together in New York. For the most part, it was good. Obviously, in the early years, there are financial strains, especially in the Big Apple. However, as an assistant principal at the Walton School, she made enough to make inroads on her student loan. So did Graham. He landed a job as an assistant prosecuting attorney, and enjoyed several promotions in the next few years. It paid well. Better yet for future years, it set him up with political friends that would eventually come in handy. At that time, he had no intention to run for mayor, but he did always have an interest in politics. His foray into elections would come just a few years later.

After eight months in the Central West End, the couple decided it was as good a time as any to get married. They wanted a New York City wedding, and looked forward to a bright future.

2

Wedding bells

The wedding itself was a memorable event. As a Catholic, Linda had hopes that they could get married in one of the small chapels of St. Patrick's cathedral. If so, she believed it would be a dream come true. When she spoke with her local priest and the monsignor at St. Patrick's, it became very possible. Yes, there was some paperwork to fill out and meetings to be had, but ultimately they set the date for the upcoming late March.

Graham was raised as a Methodist—pretty close, but he would have to take 3-4 weeks of Pre-Cana conference classes in the church, just to be aware of some of the teachings, and to better understand his fiancee's religious beliefs, which had been ingrained since grade school. Consequently, the couple attended several weeks of classes, which was relatively painless.

She had picked several of her friends from college, and one of the teachers in her school as maids of honor. By the same token, the groom had selected many of his college buddies for the wedding party. He did name one of his fellow prosecuting attorneys as his best man. The man's name was Andrew Madden. They had become fast friends after many late nights of work together.

The small chapel they had chosen was beautifully lit, and probably held only about 120 people. It made for an intimate ceremony.

And where to hold the reception? Graham and Linda looked at several fancy restaurants, but ultimately decided that their best option was the Rock Center Cafe near the skating rink of Rockefeller

Center (which would be closed by then) For starters, everyone at the wedding could walk there. After all, it was just across the street. Also, the food was good and there was plenty of room in the center of the place for dancing.

They had hired a great local photographer and there were plenty of keepsake photos--lots of the new bride and groom, but also many of the guests. The wedding party had their own spotlight, with many individual and group photos. Some featured the new bride with Graham's groomsmen. Some featured the maids of honor surrounding the new groom, who was hugging them all, as was his ingrained habit.

The band played many hits, but for the wedding dance, Linda requested a slow version of "I only have eyes for you." Perhaps it was telling that Graham had always had a wondering eye, and the new bride obviously wanted to underscore that she was now his one and only.

Afterwards, the couple reserved the wedding suite at the Plaza Hotel. Very swanky, both had to admit. By the next morning, they packed their bags and headed to Bermuda for a few well-deserved days on the beach and just enough exotica to make it interesting.

All in all, it was a wonderful week. All the guests thought the chapel and the Rockefeller Center restaurant were inspired choices. The couple took hundreds of photos of Bermuda, which was stunning in June. If they had it to do over again, both agreed they would change nothing.

3

Baptisms

Eighteen months later, their first born was christened Rose Marie at Holy Trinity Church on West 82nd. Linda preferred to have this small ceremony at her local church, rather than St. Patrick's cathedral. She had invited one of her former classmates and teacher named Robert to be the godparents.

Fifteen months later, Michael Francis was born and similarly baptized. This time, the godparents were Andrew Madden and his wife. Andy was the prosecuting attorney who had been Graham's best man at the wedding. Over the past few years, he had come to know Robert's wife and thought it would be best the honor the couple together.

In both cases, the parents invited the couples to lunch at the Luxembourg Café, which was only a few blocks away.

In their walk, Andy brought up an out-of-the-blue topic to Graham. "Ever think of running for office? "the friend volunteered.

"Me?" Graham answered.

"Yeah. I've seen you in the courtroom and in a few town halls. You've got a knack."

"Stop it," Graham advised. After a few minutes, Andy quickly answered. "You should be mayor."

"Mayor? Why don't you run?"

"Because you have more charisma. You're sexier looking. Almost like a movie star. And women really like you. A lot of them are democratic voters. Besides, I've seen you on some of the talk shows and you are a star…giving ideas about how to reduce crime and make the city more affordable.

On top of that, you know all the politicos. They like you too…and there will be an opening this year for the mayor's job."

"You think there will be?"

"Absolutely.

"Will you give it some serious thought?" Andy suggested.

"I don't know," Graham honestly answered.

"I think you'd be great. And I know dozens of people who would campaign for you…including me. Will you think about it, at least?"

After a few minutes, Graham responded. "I will think about it. Might be tough with two little kids."

"Might be easier. For one thing, your wife is going to be busy, busy. I assume she's going to take some time off from teaching."

"Yep," Graham nodded. "She thinks it may work best to take a few years off from the Walton School. I don't blame her. As a matter of fact, I think it would be good for the kids and for her.

"I would think so. Try to visualized it. You on the podium. A beautiful wife and two adorable kids on stage with you. It's irresistible!"

"I'll think about," Graham promised. "Meanwhile, let's have a brunch. Don't bring this up to Linda. It's hers and kids' day."

"Of course," Andy agreed and they followed the women and the kids into the restaurant.

4

Maybe you should run as mayor

Over the next few months, several people were rumored to be considering a race for mayor.

One was the President of the Board of Education—a 63 year old woman that was thought of as too safe for the rough-and-tumble job of mayor. There were two alderman whose names had been mentioned. Both were from the outer boroughs and were considered too bland. Neither one of them had the slightest send of humor. Also, there was the director of public works and sanitation, but no one wanted to be constantly reminded of how efficiently the trash was collected, or effectively the dirty streets were occasionally swept.

And then there was Graham's appearance on *The View*. He had been on the show five times and was usually invited when the hosts wanted to talk about justice, civic events, or government responsibilities. Despite the fact that the show had a national audience, most of the hosts also enjoyed talking about New York City.

Joy Behar started the interview by congratulating Graham and the birth of his new son.

"He's a handsome lad," Graham bragged.

"Here's hoping he has a great life ahead of him…but with all the violence out there in America's cities, it's a little iffy."

"It doesn't have to be. We just need to clamp down on police tactics, incarceration rules, and aim for a better quality of life each and every day. In a city like New York that has so much to offer, it's absolutely crazy that people can't find enough fun things to do to keep their brain off violence. In this city, there is excitement and thrills around every corner. It's not perfect from a crime standpoint, but the cops are good…and the attractions are everywhere."

"Maybe you should run as mayor of New York," Whoopi Goldberg innocently suggested.

"I've been told that," Graham answered.

"Wow, we have some news on *The View*," Whoopi reacted. "And I've got a hunch you could be quite good."

"Think so?"

"Yeah.

"Well, I love this city. I was born here. I live here. I was married here and have two kids who now represent the future of this great city. It just needs to be the crown jewel of American society."

Ok, it was a somewhat rehearsed line from Graham Kruse. It was a very repeatable line on the local news that night.

It also garnered many headlines in the *New York Times, New York Post, and the Daily News.* The typical story was that Mr. Kruse, one of the city's foremost prosecuting attorneys, had hinted that he might consider running for mayor.

Before he could exit the studio, he got a call from his wife, Linda. "First of all, you were wonderful on the show. But are you really weighing the idea of running for mayor?"

"It has crossed my mind," Graham admitted. "Graham brought it up to me as we were walking to lunch the other day. I was non-committal to him. But we should talk about it."

"You bet," she answered. "However, let me give you my first thought. Right out of the gate, I am in total support of the idea. Actually, I think the city needs you."

"You are the best," Graham replied. "Give the kids a hug."

Before he could hail a cab outside the studio, he did get a call from Andy. "Andy did you see my interview today on *The View*?

"I did," Andy awswered. You were awesome."

"Really?"

"Absolutely," Andy asserted. "I only have one key question for you, and it's a doosy. When do we start the campaign," his best man teased.

5

Talk, Talk, Talk shows

Within the next 48 hours, Graham Kruse became a media star in New York.

He was invited to appear on the Kelly and Ryan show, where he discussed the importance of sharing the city's attractions with one's children. "Take them to the Botanical Gardens and the Zoo. Every kid loves these unique parks. Besides, the spring weather is beautiful right now. But don't forget the art museum and galleries. It will help open their minds to a bigger, brighter world."

On the *Morning Joe* show, he discussed a world of opportunities for woman with Mika Brzezinski.

"I love women," he readily admitted. "I think they are smart, multi-talented, and often exhibit amazing common sense. To make this world a better place to live, we need all hands on deck, and that includes women, Blacks, Latinos, and Asian-Americans. The more we can make that a team, the more successful New York will be."

On the *Stephanie Rhule show*, he discussed the financial health of the city.

"New York City is admittedly expensive. But we need to provide financial relief for many of our private citizens. We have to limit the evictions of tenants because they miss one payment. I would be in favor of increasing the minimum wage for all city employees."

"When are you going to announce that you are actually running?" Stephanie asked.

"I'm not ready to do that yet," Graham answered.

On Andy's advice, he had agreed to avoid the actual announcement of his candidacy. According to his best friend, the moment he did so, it would immediately generate its own barrage of news reports… and there would be no turning back. Also, he needed to discuss this possible move with his wife. Linda. That night, he did so.

Two nights later, after the kids have gone to sleep, Graham turned on the coffee machine, and poured two late night cups. He then found his wife upstairs and invited her to join him in the kitchen.

"What's on your mind?" she asked.

"Have you been thinking about becoming the first lady of the city of New York," he responded

"As my husband would say, it has crossed my mind," she answered.

"And…." He waited for a response.

After a pause, she brought up one of her chief concerns. "I worry about the kids. I really do. As you know, I have resigned from the Walton School, so I can give them my attention in the early years. But it would be a lot of work on my shoulders."

Graham had anticipated this. "Well, for one thing, if I were ever to become mayor of New York, I would be home every night. Also, if it gets too much, we could get childcare help for you. Someone to ease the burden. Fact is, we should probably get that anyway."

"Maybe so," she agreed. Then she proceeded to a touchier subject. "I also worry about temptations on the campaign trail."

"What do you mean," Graham sincerely asked.

"Honey, c'mon…you would have all this time to yourself, and all these women around you. You know yourself. You like to hug and kiss people, and you even like to flirt a little. It's dangerous."

"Babe, first of all, I would not be alone all the often. I've been to the mayor's office. There is staff everywhere. Frequently, there are press people around. So I would have to behave myself."

"Would you?" she wondered out loud.

"I would certainly try to," he nodded. He leaned over and gave his wife a loving kiss and announced he would be officially running for mayor.

"If I get some childcare help, I will try to go to some campaign events. Not every night, but it might be a nice reminder to you of all you have at home."

"That would be great," they agreed. And the next week, Graham Kruse made the announcement.

6

The Race is On

After some consultation with Andy, who had decided to take a leave of absence from his prosecuting attorney's to help run the campaign, Graham announced on Friday, April 2.

Andy scrambled to find an appropriate launch site. He looked at the library in mid-town, Central Park (too iffy weather-wise), the statue of liberty (too far for most reporters), Times Square (a little too theatrical) and the courthouse (too narrow an appeal for a candidate who needed to demonstrate that he was more than just a successful attorney.

Ultimately, they settled on the Rockefeller Center walkway leading down to the skating rink. It had sentimental appeal for both Graham and Linda Kruse. Also, it was a true landmark with its annual Christmas tree lighting.

Andy invited media not just from NYC, but also from other U.S. cities since he considered this a "moment of national importance."

Graham had ordered a limo to pick up his wife and two kids an hour and half before the 1 p.m. start time. He also made sure that they had chairs for each of them on the stage just to the right of the podium. Once they arrived, he made sure that photographers could get good smiling pictures of this model family.

Finally, at 1:05, Andy approached the podium and began the proceedings. He was never a compelling speaker, but his facts and the moment gave him a little more presence.

"I am here to introduce the future mayor of New York, Graham Kruse. I have known him for several years, and am pleased to serve as his campaign manager. Let me tell you, Graham is one talented, intelligent, successful man.

"Of course, he will need to be to manage a city this diverse and large. He will administer all city services, the police and fire protection, most public agencies, and enforce all city and state laws in New City.

"How big is it? Well, the budget is the largest in the US at 100 billion, The city employs 325,000 people, and spends 21 billion to educate more than 1.1 million students. It's the largest public school district in the country, partly because we serve all five boroughs—Manhattan, the Bronx, Brooklyn, Staten Island, and Queens.

"So we need an accomplished, visionary man for this job. And that man is Graham Kruse. Please allow me to introduce him—the next mayor of New York. The one and only Graham Kruse."

There was a large round of applause, and lots of flashbulbs. Over an instrumental version of the Sinatra hit "New York, New York," the candidate waved to many people in the audience, and pointed to them as if he knew each and every one. True to form, he also threw kisses to these strangers.

After a few minutes, he gestures to silence the crowd, and began speaking.

"First of all, I want to thank you all for coming out, and send a special thanks to my campaign manager who introduced me. Thank you, Andy. I would also like to introduce my beautiful wife, Linda. Stand up Linda…let them see who you are.

And I'd like to introduce my kids—Rose Marie and Michael Francis. Stand up kids and take a bow."

"Once they were seated, Graham looked at notecards and began his address.

"I want to run for mayor of this, my hometown city, because I believe it is the best city in the world, and I believe I can make a difference here.

"We have great museums and parks, and wonderful schools. We have the best theatres, great services here, and wonderful neighborhoods in every single borough. But it can always be better… and if elected, that would be my mission in life.

"I want to make this one of the safest cities in America. From my time as a prosecuting attorney, I believe we need help the police become a more integral partner of the communities.

"I believe we need make this a more affordable place to live, especially for the middle and working classes. This should not be a place just for CEO's. No, it should be a place where people can work hard for a decent wage and not fear that they will be evicted by a landlord.

"We should make our culture more accessible.

"We should make travel in the inner city less of a jam-packed nightmare.

"We should continue to make our schools the envy of the world, and encourage more field trips so kids can get a head start in life.

"We should encourage exercise in the work place, and on weekends.

In all, Graham hi-lighted about twelve priorities. As he and Andy had discussed there should be something for everyone.

"Lastly, I want to be mayor because I think I sincerely think I can do the job, and I sincerely believe I am the best person for the job. I want to encourage all of you to participate in this effort, and talk to your friends about the true promise of this great city.

"Thank you all for attending and have a beautiful afternoon."

He then walked over to his wife and kids, gave them all a hug, and waved to everyone in the audience.

Andy joined him from the other side of the stage, and told him "Nice job." His wife said the same thing, and after waving to the gradually thinning crowd, the candidate, his family and campaign manager cleared the stage.

7

Liz and the commercial

Andy placed a call to Graham in the morning to discuss a key addition to the staff. "Her name was Liz Quinlan," the campaign manager said, and she is a well-respected public relations and advertising person."

"Is she good," the candidate asked.

"I have heard she is by far the best p. r. person in town. As a matter of fact, I quietly invited her to get all those news people and broadcasters to your announcement the other day. I figured you wouldn't mind."

"Not at all," Graham answered.

"And she was also instrumental in getting some of those TV interviews you have had over the past week or so."

"Wow. She sounds terrific. Do I owe her some money?"

"I've given her a stipend from our campaign war chest," Andy acknowledged. "But once you meet her, you may want to up the ante."

"When will I meet her?"

"I set up a meeting this afternoon at 1 p.m. She's one of the principles of a p.r. firm downtown in Greenwhich Village. Can you make it?"

"Of course," Graham answered. I look forward to meeting her."

"…and you will very much look forward to working with her," Andy predicted.

At 1:00 p.m., the two men met on 13th and 6th Avenue in front of her building.

"Would she be willing to take a leave from the communications firm to work full time on the campaign," Graham asked.

"I would think so, but if you like her, ask," Andy responded.

They walked to the fifth floor and entered the small office that housed her business. It was smart-looking and high tech—not elegantly furnished, but comfortable decorated.

The receptionist escorted the two men to the corner office. Once they entered, Andy introduced Liz.

She immediately stood up from her desk and smiled. "Well, it's nice to meet you face-to-face. I have watched a few of your TV interviews and attended your kick-off announcement. Very impressive. How can I help?"

"Join the campaign. I only hear good things about you," Graham said. He then gave her a big welcoming hug. He couldn't help but notice that she was a good-looking woman, provably in her late 20's. "I think this could be lots of fun," the candidate added.

"Important, too. People need to become more acquainted with you. They need to be comfortable seeing you on the air," the communication expert suggested.

I think in addition to the free media, we should create a commercial around your "dreams, your charisma, and your persona."

"I hope it's not a non-stop talking lecture," the candidate cautioned. "I see them on the air all the time and fall asleep. I hear music in the spot."

"We already see eye-to-eye," she said.

"Can we use that Sinatra song, 'New York, New York,' the candidate asked. "I loved hearing that in Rock Center before my kick off announcement."

"Just the instrumental. I don't want the Sinatra voice to date you and make people think you are older than you are. After all, you are a young vibrant man, and I'd rather they focus on you and what you have to say."

"I like this gal," Graham admitted and gave a thumbs up to Andy.

"I took the liberty of creating a prototype for the spot. I hope to shoot in parts of all five boroughs. I'll write the initial script with Andy's help. I think it will take about 3-4 days to complete a first draft. Of course, if any of the words are not your apropos to you, you should feel free the change it."

"Great," Graham smiled. "Should I invite my wife to participate in one of the day's shoots?"

"That would probably be a great idea, if she's willing," Liz answered.

"Well, it's great to meet you Liz, and I look forward to working with you," he said, and concluding the brief meeting with little kiss on her cheek. Nothing too, too sexy. Just his tried-and-true way to let people know he appreciates them.

* * * *

The actual commercial was completely scripted by Liz, without a single change from the candidate. It went like this:

WE OPEN IN THE CENTER OF FIFTH AVENUE, WHEN THE SINATRA LYRIC BEGINS TO PLAY. AS IT DOES, THE CANDIDATE WALKS BRISKLY AND ADDRESSES THE CAMERA.

V.O. It's my favorite city in the world. New York, New York— where almost anything is possible and dreams can come true. My name is Graham Kruse, and I am determined to make that happen if I am fortunate enough to be elected your mayor.

CUT TO A LOWER MIDDLE CLASS NEIGHBORHOOD IN THE BRONX. GRAHAM SHAKES A FEW HANDS OF AFRICAN-AMERICA WORKERS AND ADDRESSES THE CAMERA.

V.O. I intend to make this city more affordable for all hard-working people.

CUT TO GRAHAM GETTING OFF A FERRY BOAT IN STATEN ISLAND.

V.O. I want to make transportation easier for all.

CUT TO GRAHAM WALKING BY THE SILVER GLOBE NEAR THE QUEENS TENNIS COURTS.

V.O. I want you to feel on top of the world here.

CUT TO GRAHAM AT PROSPECT PARK WATCHING A KID'S BASEBALL GAME IN BROOKLYN.

V.O. And everyone should feel like a winner.

CUT TO GRAHAM JOINED BY HIS WIFE AT THE ROCKEFELLER CENTER PROMENADE. THEY HUG.

V.O. I know my wife Linda and I feel that every morning. And so do our kids who were also born here. So, we can make it happen with your help. Vote Graham Kruse for mayor of the most exciting city in the world. Thanks for your support.

THE INSTRUMENTAL OF 'NEW YORK, NEW YORK' RINGS OUT, AS MR. AND MRS. KRUSE HUG AND WALK. FADE TO BLACK.

* * * *

The commercial ran a few days later, and was only adjusted to remind people to vote in the primary.

8

The running of a campaign

The TV interviews and that commercial certainly boosted candidate Kruse's campaign.

However, as Graham and Andy realized, it was now time for some very hard work. They needed to meet with many of the direct reports and build a bridge with them all. That included the fire chief, the chief of police, transportation professionals, and various deputy mayors who had expressed no interest in running for the top office. Other important links were with the heads of the library, the Metropolitan Museum, the botanical garden, and the top officials of the Yankees, Mets, Giants, Knicks, Nets, and Rangers.

In addition to building some star power for the team, Graham and Andy needed to identify many staff members who could create position papers and help elect the candidate. In total, they believed they might need 100-200 new faces with resumes as impressive as Liz Quinlan's (who had agreed to take a leave from her p.r. firm to work full time on the campaign). The grand staffing process would entail a lot of interviewing, but it would inevitably make the candidate smarter.

In order to hone his skills, the candidate also visited the organizations where as mayor, he would be an ex-officio board member. They included:

The American Museum of Natural History

The Brooklyn Academy of Music
Carnegie Hall
Lincoln Center for Performing Arts
The Metropolitan Museum of Art
The NY Public Library
The NY Shakespeare Festival.

At each locale, he would meet with the top brass and then have a town hall on the premises, which was generally covered by the press.

His biggest internal meeting was with the comptroller, who had the full access to the purse strings of the city. He was also incredibly wired with the business leaders in the community. They seemed to hit if off, so Graham to decided to go all out and ask for the order. The candidate addressed the man with a great deal of respect. "Sir, I have two questions for you. 1. If I am elected, would you like to continue to serve? 2. Can you recommend a leader in economics who could help this campaign raise money, and keep the books straight?"

The comptroller was not interested in serving another term. "No offense, I'm just too old for four more years. But I have lots of suggestions for an exec who could help you raise money. He then took out a sheet of paper and wrote down five names with their phone numbers. "I spoke with the last guy—Martin Dimling—yesterday. He seemed to have nice things to say about you. So I would try him first."

Graham did just that. He called Martin and liked the guy's experience and enthusiasm for the campaign. Within 24 hours, he arranged a meeting with Andy and himself. Within 48 hours, they had a deal. And soon, the dollars started to flow.

9

Thank You's

The campaign visits to all those institutions where Graham would serve as a board member if elected mayor proved to be a p.r. bonanza.

Thanks to Liz Quinlan, she had arranged relevant talking points and a little press coverage for every locale. For example, at Carnegie Hall, she had constructed a sheet that suggested the importance of music and history in everyone's life—not just kids, but also grownups. For the mayoral candidate, it was easy to link this to the special advantages of New York City and promise to keep this a priority in the years ahead.

Probably 75 people attended (mostly Carnegie employees and friends of the institution. A few news folks attended too, and there would probably be a positive blurb in their next edition about Kruse's outreach to culture.

After the crowd started to thin, the candidate complimented Liz on all she was doing for the campaign. "Can I buy you a cocktail," he asked.

"I wouldn't mind one. That would be nice," she responded.

"Well, there are plenty of places near here. Let's go to the Russian Tea Room. It's just a few doors away, and always fun."

At that time of the afternoon, no reservation was necessary. They simply waltzed through the door, and took a table near the bar. Graham ordered two glasses of white wine and toasted this p.r. person. "You make me look good and smart. I really appreciate it. You know so much about me, but I have no idea how you got so brilliant."

The woman explained that she had always done well in school, but felt a special affinity for political campaigns.

"Well, you are damn good at it," Graham smiled. He then reached across the table and took her hand. He then gently kissed it. "And I appreciate all you do.

Just then, Graham's cellphone rang. It was Andy. "Hey, how did it go?" he asked. "Great," Graham answered.

"I tried to get there on time, but got held up. I'm in Carnegie Hall now and hear I just missed you."

"We're just two doors down at the Russian Tea Room having a glass of wine," the candidate said. "Come join us. I'm just complimenting Liz on a job well done. It was a good turn out."

Andy responded, "I'll be there in two minutes." In truth, it was probably only 90 seconds when he walked through the door and joined them at the table. He was curious about the press coverage of the event, and the turnout. He also wanted to give Liz some positive feedback on the commercial that he had heard from the staff people he was interviewing.

After one glass each, Graham excused himself and thought it would be a good day for a short walk back to his West Side apartment. Andy offered to taxi Liz home. All gave high fives to each other and exited the restaurant.

10

Who took the picture?

The next morning, Liz Quinlan opened the daily newspapers to see if Graham had received any positive coverage from his visit at Carnegie Hall. In the *New York Times*, there was a blurb about the candidate's visit to the hall, and a suggestion that New Yorkers take advantage of more local culture.

The *NY Post* included a picture of Graham at the podium answering some questions.

When she opened the *NY Daily News*, there was no story on page one. However, on page 3, there was a bombshell! There were two pictures of her and the candidate at a table in the Russian Tea Room. One was a picture of Graham and Liz clinking glasses of wine. In the other one, he was lifting her hand and giving it a kiss. *Omigod*, she thought. Under these two pictures there was a caption, "Is this any way a married man should run for mayor?" If she didn't have better wits about her, she might have fainted.

Obviously, she knew nothing had really happened between the two of them. But she obviously knew that pictures can be powerful.

Liz immediately called Andy and alerted him they had a major problem on their hands. She invited him to get the *NY Daily News* and turn to page 3…and then immediately call her back before calling Graham.

In fifteen minutes, Andy called back, and was in a panic. "This isn't good," he agreed.

"Who took the pictures?" she wondered.

"Could have been anyone. Maybe a supporter of another campaign, who had a cellphone. The quality of the shots don't look great, but they can do damage. He then took a deep breath. "Hey, we can all be the alibi. Nothing nasty happened. He walked home to his wife. I took you to your place in a cab. But we need to get to Graham before he gets barraged with ugly press conjectures. Let's meet at the front of his building."

"Twenty minutes?" she asked.

"See you then."

From the street, Andy called and told Graham he had to come down for an important meeting in the street.

"What's it all about?" the candidate wondered.

"Just meet us there. We have to figure out a game plan," his campaign manager urged.

When Graham joined them in the street, he looked befuddled at the bru-ha-ha. When Andy showed him the newspaper photos, the candidate shook his head in disbelief. "Holy shit," he exclaimed. "Who took these shots?"

"Nobody knows," Andy answered.

"It wasn't the press," Liz answered. "If it were, the quality would have been better."

"You know, nothing happened last night," Graham asserted.

"We all know that, but it will take all three of us to defeat this ugly insinuation," Andy answered.

"I'll schedule a noon press conference to debunk this," Liz suggested. "Until then, no talking to the press."

"Just tell me where to be," Graham replied. "But I better have a pow-wow with my wife to explain this is all bullshit."

"If it will help, I'll vouch for the fact that I myself brought Liz home," the campaign manager volunteered. "Liz, you set up the presser and let us know where and when.

With that, the candidate the campaign manager entered the apartment building and headed upstairs to discuss the potential damage (and possible solutions) with Mrs. Kruse.

* * * *

She wasn't happy. In fact, she was aghast. After a deep breath, she asked the childcare employee to take the kids to a different room and keep them occupied.

When they were clearly out of earshot, she peered into Graham with steely eyes and said, "What the hell was going on? No bullshit. Tell the truth."

Graham gestured to Andy to let him take the lead in this particular response. "Nothing was going on," the candidate asserted. "After a tough week or two, I invited her to have a glass of wine next door to Carnegie Hall to thank her for all she had done on behalf of this campaign. I have never kissed her on the lips. I have never touched her in any inappropriate places. I simply wanted to say thanks."

"So you kissed her on her hand?" his wife rebutted sarcastically.

"You know me honey," Graham said I talk with my hands."

"Well, the pictures look awful," she said, rolling her eyes.

"Can I have a word? Can I join in here?" Andy asked Graham.

"Help yourself."

"I actually joined the group just a few minutes after they entered the restaurant. I actually sat at the same table and had a glass of wine with them...but that doesn't make as good a picture. More to the point, Linda...Graham excused himself, and walked home. On the other hand, I gave Liz a lift home to her apartment. So I can testify that absolutely nothing nasty transpired."

He then explained that they were having a noon press conference to clear the air, and exonerate Kruse. "It will be me, Graham and Liz. Her testimony will be critical."

"I don't want to be there,' Linda said.

"I don't think you should be," both men agreed.

* * * *

The press conference was scheduled at noon at the Press Club in midtown Manhattan. Not surprisingly, it was filled with newsmen and photographers from all the newspapers and magazines in New York.

The three-some had agreed that some of measure of outrage was in order. However, they didn't want to come off as insanely angry. The game plan was to minimize this and make it go away.

As agreed, Liz led off the presser, since she was an ally of the press and offered the easiest, most convincing rebuttal.

"Contrary to the article and the ugly implication in the *Daily News*, nothing illicit happened. We had one glass of wine together after a long week. People do this all the time. You probably do too. He then toasted me for a job well done, wanted to thank me for helping the campaign. That's it. End of story…other than the fact that someone had a cellphone, and used to harm a good man's candidacy."

She also vouched for the fact that he had never made an untoward advance towards her. As agreed with the two gentlemen, she was not going to outline his positions—just deny any ugly suggestions, and pass it along to the candidate.

Graham took the podium and was shaking his head in disbelief. "Perhaps this is why good people refuse to get into public service. They are smeared, and unjustly accused of wrongdoing. I simply wanted to share a glass of wine with a key woman who has contributed so much to this campaign. It was my first glass of wine with her. If you have seen the picture, I was smiling because I wanted to thank her for all she had done for this campaign.

"Incidentally, nothing nasty has ever happened between us. As many of you know, I am happily married with two kids. And nothing with my business associate Liz is about to change that…as my campaign manager can attest to. Andy?"

With that, Andy came to the podium and made it clear that he could affirm the innocence of the evening. "I arrived at the restaurant about three minutes late, but early enough to have a glass of wine with them. As to the purity of the night, I can attest that Graham in fact left early—by himself, I might add—to get a little exercise and walk home to his apartment.

"I agreed to give Liz a lift to her apartment, which is near mine in the opposite direction from Graham. So if you're looking for an explanation, that's it. It was a 25 minute glass of wine between three people who work together day in and day out. Nothing more. Nothing less. Question?"

There were a few:

"Are you angry at the *Daily News*?"
"Do you plan to sue?"
"Do you imagine a backlash from women?"
"Why were you kissing her hand?"

The first three were easy denials. Graham took the last question and reiterated that was not intended as a naughty gesture. "I just wanted to say thank you…and as some of you know, I occasionally talk with my hands and gestures."

The rumors died in the next few days. A week later, Kruse did suffer a slight dip in his popularity (two points). However, within 48 hours, he also retained his 8-point lead against his nearest competitor.

11

The Primary

The Democratic primary on June 18 attracted a fair amount of press interest. As a largely democratic city, the winner normally has a decided edge over the Republican candidate. Consequently, many of the newspapers focus on the race between rivals in the D column.

Graham, Andy and Liz were pleased that three newspapers had endorsed Kruse. The *New York Times* called him "the right man for the times" and outlined many of his popular positions. The *New York Post* dubbed him "intelligent and charismatic enough to benefit the city." The *Village Voice* thought he could bring "some cool class to an otherwise preoccupied, P & L city."

Only the *Daily News* dissented. Rather than refer to any of the past stories they had run, they endorsed Brian P. Conrad, the head of health in the city and the only acknowledged gay candidate in the race. As of primary day, he was polling as the least popular choice.

"Figures," Andy reflected. "They wanted to be 180 degrees away from their embarrassing photo and caption. Gutless!"

That afternoon, the campaign trio made several appearances near important polling places. Graham got Times Square. Andy volunteered for Queens. Liz took care of Brooklyn. Each had brochures about the candidate, and volunteered to answer any questions. By now, most voters had made up their minds, and that felt positive for the team.

By 7:30 p.m., the votes began to come in and the initial tallies looked good. By 9 p.m., most reports had Kruse comfortable ahead. By 9:30, as planned, Graham, Linda and the kids were poised to give a positive spin on the day. It was arranged in the courtyard of the Lincoln Center for Performing Art, which was well lit and set up with a stage podium, and chairs for the family.

In total, there were probably more than 50 media mavens there with cameras. Right on schedule, Adam took the podium and made a short introductions. "Ladies and gentlemen… let me introduce the next mayor of New York City—the honorable Graham Kruse.

Graham walked the podium and motioned for the crowd to hold their applause. "Well, it's still a little early, and the votes are still being tabulated, but I hear it is looking good. So I want to thank everyone for their wonderful support during this campaign. All the volunteers that made calls. All people who printed the materials that explained our positions. All the media folks who took this campaign seriously, and gave us needed air time. I even want to thank my opponents who inevitably made me better.

"But most of all, there are several special folks I want to thank. Foremost among them is Andrew Madden, who took a leave from his job as prosecutor to be my campaign manager. Also, Liz Quinlan, the p.r. pro who has made all kinds of connections with broadcasters and journalists…and also helped create the commercial with that famous Sinatra melody.

"Hey, I want to thank my family—my kids Rose Marie. Stand up and take a bow, Rose. And my son Michael. Your turn for a bow, Mike. These kids have put up with my absences and put a big smile on their face and my face whenever I could spend time with them.

"But the very most of all, I want to thank my dear wife, Linda. She has been a rock and my fiercest advocate ever since we met in college. She has been in my corner ever since I announced. In fact I wouldn't have announced, if she had not encouraged it.

"And when I would sometimes be tired after a long day of it, she would remind me that it's all worth it. The people are counting on you, she would say. You have to be there day after day for them.

"What a woman. I got lucky the day I met you, Honey. You have done nothing but make me better…and I appreciate how much energy that must take, knowing me…but also because we have two kids and she keeps focused and happy.

"So I am blessed. Come join me here, my dear."

She joined Graham on stage and gave him a big kiss. He held up her hand as if she was the champion.

Graham closed with this bit of humility. "Now, it's not over yet, but for those supporters of mine, lets keep our fingers crossed and watch the nightly news."

"I know we'll be watching," Linda volunteered an impromptu line.

"And I'll be right there on the sofa with you, hopefully smiling at the tallies and looking forward to a bright tomorrow." With that, the Sinatra instrumental started playing and Graham and Linda waltzed around the stage.

OK, it may have been a little overboard on the Linda accolades, but both Andy and Liz had urged him to praise her as much as possible in view of the recent *Daily News* snafu.

* * * *

By 11 p.m., all the local networks had called the race a victory for Graham Kruse. Most had attributed it to his ability to communicate and offer optimism for the city. In celebration, they each poured each other a glass of white wine and toasted each other for the victory.

12

The President visits

There was still a general election to run, but the odds seems stacked in Graham's favor, especially in a largely Democratic metropolitan area. His Republican opponent, a banker named Rufus T. Morgan, was a relative unknown who had none of the media savvy the Kruse.

Just to tilt things further in Graham's favor, the President of the United States, a former Ohio Democratic Senator named Lance Weiss, offered to visit the Big Apple and help campaign for Mr. Kruse. Graham immediately embraced the idea, and asked the President when he might be thinking of visiting.

"Well, since the general election is November 2, I was thinking sometime in October," the President said.

Perfect," Graham agreed. "Are there were any special issues or locations that he would like to include? Otherwise, I will gladly supply an itinerary long before you arrive," the Democratic candidate offered.

"Nope, "the President answered. "I would like a two-hour meeting with you just to discuss issues that may be of interest to both of us… but other than that, the itinerary is your call. Wait, let me think… are there any cool things going on in New York City in October?"

"There are cool things going on in New York every day," Graham proudly proclaimed. "I'll think of some things that might interest you…and a good place to draw a crowd, if either one of us wants to say a few words."

"I probably will," the President laughed.

"I can guarantee you, I will too," the mayoral candidate agreed.

In the meantime, there was plenty of campaigning and organizing to do…but given the seemingly lopsided contest, it could all be done in a more methodical, less frantic way. At least once a week, Adam and Graham would meet with all the existing deputy mayors to ascertain the state of the city. They would also meet with the chief appointees to get and give feedback for the weeks ahead.

Liz had organized a few town hall, at least once every few weeks, and in various boroughs to make all the non-Manhattan people feel engaged. And of course, there were always the media interviews… but given the pace of the campaign, this normally amounted to only one a week.

As they approached the fall season, the dynamic trio decided it was good to draft an itinerary for the Presidential visit. Graham urged that it not be stuffy, since the President himself had wanted to see some sights. The mayor continued. "Besides, we will have two hours to get serious about issues of joint interest to Washington D.C. and New York City. Adam and Liz, please put some thought into what some of those topics may be so I don't come off like a total idiot."

"Will do," they both agreed.

Liz actually suggested that if the President was amenable, perhaps they could have that meeting the evening before and follow it with a one-on-one dinner. "That way, you guys can get to know each other better, and we can have the bulk of the next day for fun…and publicity."

"Great idea," Graham agreed.

Soon enough, the agreed upon dates, October 14-15, came up on the calendar. Not surprisingly, the President took Air Force One, and was escorted to Manhattan with secret service. Graham had set up a small meeting room and dinner at the Princeton Club for privacy.

At 5 p.m. the President arrived and called Graham set up the tete-a-tete. It would be in one of the smaller offices at the Princeton Club, set up with a phone, a computer and a TV, and a variety of beverages and coffee.

President Weiss arrived at 6 p.m and the two men began to talk about shared interests. From the President's perspective, a lot of it had to do with immigration (especially through the NY airports). He also wanted to discuss a better relationship between Wall Street and his own commerce department. In addition, he hoped their could be better race relations in America's urban cities, including New York.

None of these were surprises for Graham. His two primary advisors had predicted these topics would come up, among others.

For his part, Graham wanted to discuss the almost insurmountable cost of college, especially in America's most expensive city. "Anything your education or commerce departments can do to ease the burden?"

"I'll check with them," President Weiss promised.

Other issues: Mass transit, especially between these two metropolitan areas. and the importance of childcare, especially for working women.

"All good topics," the President complimented Graham. "Food for thought. Speaking of food, I say we have dinner and put these issue on the back burner. I am looking forward to our visit to the city tomorrow. The itinerary looks fun."

"I can almost guarantee it will be. There's no need for long speeches. A five minute hello to the press would be fine. And by the way, would it be o.k. for my wife to join us at our last stop at The South Street Seaport. There's a big Oktoberfest celebration there this week end—food, drink, music, and I think she would love to see it."

"I'd love to meet her," the President proclaimed.

The dinner was an easy treat for both men. Chicken teriyaki, fresh peas, butternut squash, and a dessert of fresh sliced carrot cake. The two men did share some white wine and stories about their early years. All in all, it was a fun, easy evening, which wrapped around 9:15.

Both men agreed to meet at the Museum of Modern Art at 9:30 the next morning. Graham kicked it off by welcoming the President and briefly stressing the importance of art in our daily life. President Weiss talked about how much he enjoyed his dinner with Graham the night before and the thrill he had everyday enjoying the fine art in the White House.

Next stop: the Library. Both men agreed that learning is forever thing. "Don't think just because you 've got a college degree, you don't to read another book.

Next stop: the Museum of science. The President stressed that science will help set this country apart in the coming decades. "And that's why we a good grounding of this discipline in our grade and high schools, Graham added.

They also stopped in Wall Street and Times Square, where President Weiss enjoyed a fresh NY hot dog from one of the vendors. Both men predicted it would be in the newspapers tomorrow.

Final stop: Pier 15 at the South Street Seaport, where Linda joined her husband. President Weiss was very impressed with the large crowd and the exciting culture around every turn. He was also very thrilled to meet Mrs. Kruse. "I understand you thought this might be fun."

"I've been meaning to come for years."

"Well, this seems like a good time to be here—at the end of my tenure as President, and hopefully, the beginning of your husband's second term as New York City mayor."

"Hopefully," she agreed.

As Liz had prearranged, she asked the German band to take a break around 5 p.m. to accommodate the President and the mayor, both of whom wanted to say a few words. She had set up a podium and, as usual, invited many members of the press.

Andy went to the microphone first, and introduced the candidate Kruse and President Weiss. "The President would like to say a few words," he told the packed pier.

The President took the stage, and addressed the crowd. "What a great city you have here. And what a great mayor! We spent all day today going from one attraction to the next. A lot of people know me. But it seems like everyone here in New York City knows Mayor Kruse.

"I guess that's because he is so primed to do a great job. Oh, and I love being here for Oktoberfest. I don't know if the mayor knew, but my grandparents came to United States from Germany." He then looked at Mayor Kruse, who was holding both thumbs up.

"So who told you?" President Weiss asked the mayor.

Graham responded, "Your secretary. "When she saw Oktoberfest on the itinerary I sent, she figured you might get a special kick out that stop. the itinerary.

The President gave a thumbs up to the mayor. "So. as you have just heard, all this culture is in my blood, and I am so happy to participate. I am also pleased to endorse Graham Kruse for mayor. He's a good man, and he will be a great asset, and do a great job for this city. Ladies and Gentlemen, let me introduce the future mayor of New York City—Mayor Kruse.

When Graham went to the podium, he and the President locked hands and held the up in the air in a victory gesture. Then the mayor saluted the President and began speaking.

"Thank you, Mr. President. You have done a great job for this country, and I truly do appreciate your support. As many of you know, I am a fan of this city every single day, and for every single celebration—whether it be St. Patrick's Day, Martin Luther King day, the 4th of July, Columbus Day, or Oktoberfest. We are a very diverse city, and that's one thing that makes New York so great. So remember to go and vote on November 2. But while you are here, have some fun, some bratwurst, and perhaps even a beer—if you are over 21."

There was little chuckle over his last line, followed by applause. Graham treated his wife, the President, Andy and Liz to a Beck's beer, just as the German band began to play again.

It ended up being a wonderful night, and a very successful trip. Both the President and the mayor seemed to enjoy each other's company and share some visions for the future. In addition, there were lots of photos and press coverage that would endure many days. Finally, at 7 p.m., the limo and secret service came for the President and he was off again for Air Force One.

As Graham waved goodbye, he, Andy, Liz and Linda high-fived each other.

"Mission accomplished," they all agreed.

13

The General Election

The residual impact of the President's visit with Graham Kruse lasted for many weeks. As a matter of fact, Liz even re-edited the commercial to include President Weiss and the candidate chumming around New York, and even sharing a bratwurst.

According to the polls, the Kruse now had a 12 point lead over Rufus Morgan, the Republican candidate. It had increased each week after the Presidential visit. Rufus was a lackluster candidate, but kept talking about "winning the smart New Yorkers" (meaning the rich New Yorkers).

He was lobbying for a debate (or two or three). He even shared this with some of his few media interviews. Both Andy and Liz advised against it. "What do you have to gain debating a relative unknown? He's running out of contributions and wants to use your popularity to boost his ego."

Graham agreed. Better to just keep the campaign moving ahead and then swamp him in the general. Months passed with this strategy, but as sure as the calendar, the big election came soon enough.

All the major newspapers endorsed the democratic candidate. On November 2nd, the polls opened at 10 a.m. throughout the five boroughs. The exit polls shows Kruse with a substantial lead, and many TV stations were hinting it was over on the 6 p.m. Some wanted Graham to give a victory address at that time, but he demurred, thinking it would suggest premature braggadocio.

By the time of the 11 p.m. news, all newspapers had absolutely declared Graham the victor. Reluctantly, he agreed to give a short statement outside his apartment.

The candidate did his best to give an understated reaction. "As many of you know, I don't like to jump the gun before all the votes have been counted. It is, after all, the American way. But I am told it looks very promising. If so, I would like to take a minute to thank all the people who campaigned for me, and invite all citizens of New York to stay tuned for the final results. If it ends up in my favor, I will have more to say tomorrow. Thank you very much." With that the candidate took a bow, and exited.

Thirty minutes later, Rufus the Republican conceded the election and wished mayor-elect Kruse good wishes.

By the next morning, all the votes were counted. All the newspapers declared Kruse the winner. All the morning talk shows (even the national ones gave the same verdict.

Later on that afternoon, the new mayor gave a stem-winding address outlining his priorities, and specifically thanking all the hard-working pros who made it possible.

14

On the Job

Acch, now here comes the hard part.

Within the first few weeks on the job, Graham had a hunch that campaigning was going to be more fun than actually governing. For one thing, as a candidate all you need to do is promise things—almost as many things as you want. Once you are truly elected, you have to deliver, at least on a few things.

Just to make things more complicated, he had a feeling it was going to be a very lonely job.

Andy had just told him that he was planning to go back to the law firm. "Hey, all I did was take a leave of absence to help you get elected. Now it's time to go back to what I know."

"You can't leave," Graham gasped.

"I need a real job," Andy protested.

"But I need you here to help me in the real job." Graham answered. "Wait, Wait, wait…let me think. I can give you a real job that would be right up your alley. Deputy Mayor in charge of criminal justice! There! It could pay a quarter of a million a year. Honest!"

"I don't know, "Andy answered.

"Yes, you do. You don't want to go back and just do what you were doing before…without me."

"Let me think about it," Andy said.

"Come by tomorrow. We'll talk."

The bigger blow came from Graham's wife, Linda, who sincerely believed it would not be good for the family to move to Gracie Mansion.

"But I have to be here every day."

"And so you should…but this is no place for two kids. They need to be around friends their own age. They need to be near swing sets and carousels. Not a bunch of beaurocrats," she soberly asserted.

"But how would that work," the new mayor innocently asked.

"We'll visit you on the weekends. Or you come back to the Upper West Side on weekends. But having these kids live in a museum will not work for them, or me…or even you."

"Omigod," Graham sputtered. "I hate the thought of this," And then he looked out the window of his new office for almost a minute in silence. Eventually, he turned back to his wife. "I hate to admit it, but you may be right. Let's try to make it work your way, but I will be very lonely."

"Yeah, so don't go fooling around," she warned him.

"No, we're going to be a real family every weekend. Yikes!" the thought of it depressed him, but he had to agree the limited time did make sense.

And if that's not enough, he had to come up with a select few major projects that make a mark on this city. Not a laundry list of things, like a candidate may offer. No, these had to be just a couple doable priorities.

He thought about all the issues he had discussed in his campaign speech and narrowed it to two.

His first priority had to do with education. Even in his meeting with the President, he had suggested that the price of higher education was a major burden for people living in this expensive city.

In trying to alleviate the problem, he called in his new deputy mayor of education and the deputy mayor of commerce and taxation. He presented the problem and asked both of them for suggestions. Meanwhile, he would be thinking of ways to ease the financial burden of New York City citizens.

Their best idea? Relief from the dozen or so junior colleges in New York City.

Graham loved the fact that it encouraged high school grads to continue their education. Most of the schools were 2-year curriculums, so that could be an easier financial fix.

What the mayor liked best about the idea was that it had a creative angle to it. A lot of those schools dealt with the arts—the Academy of Dramatic Arts, the Fashion Institute of technology, the New York Film Academy. Of course, there were 2-year junior colleges with more traditional classes, but sexier schools would certainly play well in speeches and was more characteristic of the new mayor's appeal.

They were not free, but Graham proposed keeping the tuition at around $5000, and making it a one time expenditure, as opposed to a two year payment. He also worked out with his deputy mayors a plan that a student could take ten years to pay it off if they had to borrow. Meanwhile, the schools would get a tax credit.

That was proposal #1. It would take a few years to bring it to fruition. But the mayor believed it would be worth it.

However, the mayor also needed idea #2.

He always had a certain fascination and affinity for women. In fact, he learned that in the election that approximately 70% of all women voted for him. He wondered how they fared in the workplace compared to men. Through research, he discovered that women only comprised 42.8% of the managerial and professional workforce, ranking New York 9th in the nation. Worse yet, 26.8% of all women worked in low wage jobs.

Ah yes, but how to get more women in the workforce?

With the help of his Deputy Mayor of Commerce and taxation, they devised a plan that would reward companies that had an employee ratio of about 50/50. The mayor's office would give those enlightened companies a city tax break. It might even be offset with the extra city taxes that these new women employees would pay.

So it was a win-win situation.

This too would take several years to completely enact. But Graham liked both ideas and believed they could benefit the citizenry. They played to important segments of his audience. He also instinctively knew they would make great talking points in any news or interview program. Consequently, they became his priorities for his first term.

15

The Fling

After several months in Gracie Mansion, Graham found that he was incredibly lonely on weekday nights.

On the weekends, he could see his wife Linda and the kids, but it was usually at his apartment in the Upper West Side.

Graham tried to occupy his evening hours by studying the dossiers from his deputy mayors. Every once in a while, the family would come for a weekend at the Mayor's official residence, but there wasn't that much for them to do at East 88th and East End Avenue, as his wife had predicted. So instead, Graham would go back to his family apartment on the West Side. If he had an important government appointment on the weekend, he would normally attend and then return to his family afterwards.

However, that still left Monday through Friday. Not surprisingly, the days were jam-packed, but even the most dedicated workers would leave by 7 or 8 p.m. Then there would only be a few security people down the corridor in a wing far away from the mayor's office.

This was where the deputy mayors put together their progress reports every month. Sometimes, their secretaries would stay late and type them up. Wow, that sounds like evening fun! For a while, he would plug in a movie for pure escapism, but he found himself watching encore performances from premieres he had seen decades ago.

No, what he missed was human interaction.

One solution was to have a few more early evening meetings. Both of his major initiatives had been exposed to the public and the press and were well-received, but there were still details to be worked out.

One of the things that bedeviled him was why women were such a minority of the workforce. He researched the employment firms in the city to determine who had the best record of female placements and hires. He discovered that Bingham, Feiner and Cassidy on the lower East Side was the premier agency in that regard. Consequently, one morning after a slow evening, he called the number and asked to speak with one of the principles.

Her name was Nora Bingham, and she was honored to take the call from Mayor Kruse. He explained his priority to put more women to work in New York City.

"I am well aware, "she responded

"Well, I want to pick your brain as to why this imbalance exists."

"Lots of reasons," she answered.

"Well, I wonder if you could share some of your thoughts with me here at Gracie Mansion. I have a free time at 6:30 p.m. today."

"I will be there," she said and took down the address and the mayor's direct line in case she got detained.

Almost immediately after the phone call, Graham felt more positive. He took a quick shower and even put on some after shave. In about 30 minutes, Nora arrived and he greeted her with a hug and a kiss on the cheek.

"Wow, you look even younger in person," she started the conversation. Instinctively, the mayor knew he was going to like this meeting. He immediately invited her to take one of the wing chairs around the coffee table. In advance, he had asked the kitchen to prepare a carafe of coffee with two cups and some finger sandwiches.

He poured her a cup and thanked her for making this visit on short notice.

"It's my honor, and my pleasure," she said with a smile.

Graham discovered that, while childcare was a factor in lower paying jobs, it was not such a big thing in more upper level positions. That was the focus of her placement firm, and it was probably the more positive spin for the mayor's agenda.

After all, he could make childcare a priority in his second term. Right now, he wanted the secret to equalizing the workforce.

"At the more professional, managerial level, many of the people who hire are men. Typically, they want someone who is just like themselves. A sort of mini-me," she suggested.

"Wow, I don't feel that way at all," Graham said.

"That's because you are special," Nora complimented him.

Again, he smiled and asked her to continue.

"The other thing is, women need to know how to interview better, and we spend a lot of time prepping our candidates on the best way to present themselves," she proffered.

"I'll bet you are good at it," he said.

"We try to be."

After a pause, Graham wanted a slight change of subject. "Tell me about you," he said. "How did you get in this business?"

"Oh, I got out of college, and got married right away. Too quick. Got divorced in a year, and then started this firm with some friends. Been at it ever since."

"Wow, but it has been a success story," the mayor asserted. "Care for a glass of wine. Let's toast to more success. and another meeting here where I can learn more about women in business." He opened a bottle from his small refrigerator and poured two glasses. They clinked then the two of them walked to the window to see the snowstorm that have begun to blanket the lawn outside.

Nora shivered, and then remarked "Wow, it looks cold out there."

"I think it's only supposed to last all night," he quipped and gave her a hug for warmth.

After another sip, she looked at the mayor and said, "I should probably get on my way soon. You probably have other meetings, and I live all the way across town. It will take me over an hour and a half to get there."

After another sip, Graham answered. "You're my last meeting of the day. Why drive yourself crazy in this traffic? Why don't you just stay here?"

After a moment, Nora smiled and said, "I may take you up on that. She then leaned over and gave him a kiss. And that was the start of a very memorable evening.

It was the first time in many years that Graham had sex with anyone other than his wife. He had to admit to himself it was fun exploring a different body. They both had their share of giggles and vowed to have another such meeting someday in the not too distant future.

Given their schedules, it would be three weeks before their next meeting at Gracie Mansion. This time, Nora brought some print outs to deal with the topic of women in the workplace. She also brought a small bag holding a change of clothes for afterwards.

Her main message was that women interview better when they act like themselves, i.e., don't try to act like a man. Act like a woman. As she liked to say, "that's our point of difference." `

"And you do such a damn good job of it," he quipped, as he poured two glasses of white wine. Looking out the window, he said, "Well, we don't have the snow to blame tonight."

"We don't need anyone to blame," she rebutted and gave him a passionate kiss on the lips.

Within minutes, they were in bed and completely disrobed. Again, it was night of new exploratories, coupled with new giggles. As he did last time, Graham promised he would supply transportation in the a.m., so she would not miss a morning meeting.

There were three more "meetings" which took the mayor to his forty-month mark in office. As he reluctantly explained to Nora, he would have to take a hiatus for a while if he hoped to campaign again for a second term. "On the campaign trail, it's a full time job, day and night."

"I totally understand. Call me when you win," she said, and gave him a long passionate "until we meet again" kiss.

16

Carla calls

Four months later, the shit hit the fan.

Linda got a call from an old college chum named Carla Moore, who explained that she now worked for New York City.

"Carla, yes, I remember you from one of our business courses. What are you up to?" Linda asked innocently. "I actually work in Gracie Mansion, and have been stewing for many months about whether to call you or not."

"Well, I am glad you called. You know my husband just got elected to a second term," she beamed.

"Yes, I do…and that's why I didn't call immediately. I didn't want to put you in a difficult position, but I ended up thinking that if it were me, I would want to know."

"Want to know what," Linda asked.

Carla explained that she had all the records of the ins and outs of Gracie Mansion. She also explained that a woman came to visit the mayor five times towards the end of his first term. She would come in at the end of the workday and leave in the following morning.

"Holy shit," Linda said.

"I wasn't in the mayor's office. I was down the corridor in a different wing, but that's a long visit from a woman and a recurring one. Mind you, I haven't shared this information with anyone in the mayor's office Deep down, it just seemed very suspicious to me, unless it was maybe a sister of the mayor."

Linda got the name of the mayor's visitor, and admitted it was not Graham's sister. She then thanked Carla for the information.

For the longest time, she just stormed back and forth in her living room. Finally, she took a deep breath, and made several business and legal calls. When she felt she had ammunition, she called her husband the next morning at Gracie Mansion.

"Graham...Linda. You've got some splainin' to do. My suggestion? Get your ass back to the Upper West Side asap. I'll explain when you get here."

Quite honestly, she had never spoken to him this way before.... so he knew something was up. He asked his secretary to cancel all meetings for the day, and was promptly driven to his West Side apartment.

When she explained what she knew, he said, "Holy shit."

"That's exactly what I said." Linda answered.

Graham dropped his head, and considered what his next words should be. Instinctively, he knew it would be futile to deny the affair with Nora.

"Look, I admit it happened four or five times, but we were both consenting adults. The last thing I wanted to do was hurt you, Linda."

"Well, you did," she rebutted.

"And it hasn't happened for months. It was a brief fling. And nothing has happened since."

There was silence on he part of Linda.

After a few minute, Graham ventured into the dark beyond. "So what do you think we should do about it?" he innocently asked.

"I have already spoken to a lawyer about getting a divorce."

"Omigod," Graham had to catch his breath. Honey, we don't need to take that step."

Again, his wife was silent for several, excrutiating seconds. Then she spoke quietly, but firmly. "I've thought about this for several days, through tears late at night, and I think it is the only path forward. The thing is, for the sake of the children, I don't want a long, strung out battle. It's not good for me. It's not good for Rose Marie or Michael."

"I hear you," the mayor finally responded.

Linda continued. "So I have a deal for you—we announce that we have decided to part ways mutually with no further explanations. Not an excuse from you. Not an accusation from me. Not a screaming, shouting match in a divorce court…or in the press. It could be quick and clean."

"How quick?" he was afraid to ask, but knew he needed to.

"My lawyer suggest that if we can agree to terms, we might be able to move forward in four to six months."

"Anything else?" he asked.

"Yes, in exchange for that generosity on my part, I expect a large financial settlement. We will never discuss the amount in public… but I have spoken with a financial advisor and he has given me a ballpark idea of what it would take to keep this household afloat, poised for the future… and keep your name out of ugly headlines."

"Do the kids know anything about this?" he asked.

"No, and I want to keep it that way."

For a few moments, Graham sat in the familiar living room in silence. Then a tear rolled down his cheek. "Honey, I am so sorry."

"Yeah, well perhaps you should have thought about these things before fucking around in your office."

More tears came from the eyes of the mayor. He asked if he could wash his face before leaving. As he stood by the door, he shook his head, partly not believing this turn of events, but mostly not believing his own behavior.

"I just want to say again," he began.

"I know…you are sorry," she completed the sentence. She too shook her head in disbelief.

For a few seconds, the couple just stared at each other. Finally, Graham broke the silence. "I guess I should get a lawyer," he said.

"To each his own. I only repeat that I don't want an ugly challenge that will only hurt the kids…perhaps permanently."

With that, Graham feebly waved goodbye.

The moment he was out the door, Linda took a deep breath and started crying again as she had done every night.

17

Turning the Page

Graham Kruse had every reason to believe that the months ahead would be very different from the years before. Of course, the biggest change would be that his marriage had gone POOF.

When he got back to his office, he called his best friend Andy Madden (who had fortunately decided to take the job as Deputy Mayor of Criminal Justice) and explained the situation on the home front. Andy advised him to keep a low profile on this subject. "Yeah, you will need a lawyer, but hopefully not a combative one...because it sounds like Linda has a very good instinct on this, for you, for her, for the kids."

"I guess so," Graham reluctantly agreed.

The next day, he called Nora and told her that he had all the information he needed from her, and wouldn't need any future meetings.

"Really?" she said with some disappointment in her voice.

"Yes, really," the mayor said definitely.

Ultimately, he decided that creating some new priorities for his second term could be the only thing that might keep him sane. Given his situation on the home front (and the possible backlash if the true story ever got out), he decided that a childcare initiative could offer him a life raft. For starters, it would appeal to the lower wage women who voted for him. Moreover, it could also give these young New Yorkers a head start in life.

To get things started, he asked his deputy mayor for education how they might institute a program that could provide stimulation and social skills for pre-kindergarten kids. Question: should it be limited to pre-school? Should that be viewed as a starting point? His worry was that if he extended it to fifth graders, the price would be prohibitive, even with government assistance. He believed that perhaps it would be enough to get some plan on the books for the pre-K. One step at a time, he suggested to his deputy mayor Education.

At the time, he was stumped as to what his second priority could be. The more time he spent with Andrew, the more he wished it could have something to do with criminal justice. Given the fact that they both came from the same background, It would ideal again to work as a team.

Ultimately, they decided that it was important to improve the reputation of the police departments.

For starters, he believed a bigger percentage of the police officers should come from the neighborhoods of their precincts (as of now, many came from different locales). Together, they believed at least some portion of the police department's day should be devoted to community service. Perhaps it could be 10% or less. It could build bridges with the local teenagers and perhaps signal that cops could be their friends.

Andy particularly liked this idea and promised to research it with several local departments.

Like the priorities in Kruse's first term, the research and details of both these initiatives would take months, but the mayor believed that both had merit. Besides, it would keep him from obsessing about his upcoming divorce every hour of the day.

His attorney, a mutual friend of both he and Andy, advised him that he would pursue three priorities in this case.

1. Keep it out of the headlines.
2. Encourage a speedy settlement. The lawyer explained that it would help if neither party contests too much.
3. Argue strongly that Graham should have visitation rights with the kids.

"Will it be every weekend as it is now?" the mayor asked.

Arnold Barnes, the attorney answered, "Not likely, but you don't want to get shut out. That would look very, very incriminating. At the very least, it should be once a month…probably based from Gracie Mansion. If you think it's best for the kids, take that weekend and visit the mountains or the ocean from Long Island, or the farmlands in upstate New York. It might even be fun for you, and it will make it easier to be close to the kids."

Graham shook his head in agreement, understanding the appeal of such a plan. Then he launched into dollars and cents. "Ok, now the hard part. Linda says she is looking for a handsome financial settlement."

"Most women do," Arnold the attorney agreed.

"What do you suggest?" the mayor asked.

"I have an associate who is an excellent financial wizard. I think you should visit with him and open your books. Include everything—investments, home equity, and inheritance. This will be painful, but it all needs to be on the table. I can assure you that her attorneys will insist on that."

"Ouch!"

"Her attorneys will also want to factor in the kids' projected educational expenses through high school and even college."

"Double ouch!" Graham reacted.

Arnold the attorney then did his best to prepare the mayor for a big number. "It will probably be more money than you anticipate."

"And that doesn't even factor in your fee," Graham quipped.

The attorney could only laugh. "Believe me, my fee will be a pittance compared to the checks you will have to write to untangle yourself from this mess."

"I may not even have enough money to ever go on a date again," Graham sighed.

Arnold laughed again. "After this ordeal, you may not want to."

18

Tackling crime

After several meetings between the mayor and his deputy mayor, both men began that believe that building a bridge between the NYPD and the local communities was going to be more difficult than they originally thought.

Andrew Madden, the deputy mayor of criminal justice began his research by visiting many of the police precincts throughout the city. He discovered that improving morale was going to be more difficult than having more cops visiting the local YMCA, schools and boys clubs down the street. Yes, that would help…but he began to believe that there were bigger burning issues.

Despite the fact that the NYPD is the largest force in the nation, it is hardly representative of the true population of the city or even the state. It is a largely White department in a very diverse city. The force has 4700 officers, but only 4% are Black and only 6% are Hispanic. (compared with 16% and 19% statewide). Is it any wonder that the local community does not feel a kinship with the cop on the beat?

"Wow," Mayor Kruse reacted. "That's a serious gap."

Andy agreed. "I'm not sure how to address it without critisizing the various precincts that obviously favor White prospects. That will just destroy morale and make attitudes even worse."

"Yeah," the mayor added. And despite our size, many of the precincts are actually shorthanded, given a population of 85 million people. Trouble is, it doesn't mirror the make-up and diversity of the city."

Both men just shook their head at this dilemma. It was not an easy problem to solve.

After a few minutes, Graham teased at a possible solution. "Do you know how many of our White officers are 55 or older?"

"No, but I'll bet I can find out in a week's time."

"Let's start there. No need to fire anyone. Natural attrition will create openings."

"Yeah, but how do we fill it with more Blacks and Hispanics." The deputy mayor asked.

"I've got an idea. We advertising directly to these minority communities and let them know that this city needs them in the police department. I'll bet Liz could create a dynamite commercial or two that could attract Blacks and Latinos to earn respect and a good salary when they help keep this city safe by putting on a police uniform."

"That's a fantastic idea," Andy gushed. "I can see why you make the big bucks."

* * * *

Within a week, Andy had the figures. About 13% of the White staff would reach retirement age in the next 24 months.

And Liz came in a prototype commercial. Her recommendation? Make these minorities feel welcomed.

"The pitch should come from the mouths of police officers. If it's aimed at Blacks, there should be five or six black cops in the spot… but there should also be three or five white officers." Example:

> Black cops: "It's a good job."
> "You get to keep citizens safe."
> "You keep the traffic moving."
> "You cut down on crime."
>
> White cop: "And we need you."
> Black cops: "it pays well."
> "And it's a job that earns respect."
>
> White cop: "Why not apply"
> Black cop: "It could be the most important job
> You'll ever have."

Liz continued. "We run it only in Black-oriented media (although it's hard to miss who we are targeting). And we will do the same sort of thing in Latino media…with a little Spanish thrown in for good measure."

Both men applauded.

"We won't need this for a few months. Maybe even a year. We have to find some openings first. Graham shook her hand. "But it's a winner. And it doesn't even require that Sinatra instrumental. And you, my dear friend, can shoot it."

"When the time comes, I would be delighted to," she said, bowed and exited the room.

Both men looked at each other and gave a thumbs up in unison.

19

The Verdict

It had been a twelve-year marriage, with many good years, but with the gavel of the judge, the Graham and Linda's marriage was now officially over. Fact is, all the details were worked out between the divorce attorneys from each side. The judge simply had to read the documents, agree and officiate.

It was called a divorce by mutual consent. No nasty behavior or incidents were included in the documents. According to the terms, both parents had agreed to "joint custody" of the children. Linda would get them during the week and on the first three weekends of the month. On the last weekend of the month, Graham would get them, picking them up at 5 p.m. on Friday and returning them by late evening Sunday night. I suppose in a court of law that is technically called "joint custody."

He also agreed to take the kids one full week during the summer, just in case Linda wanted to take a vacation with some adult friends.

The kids, who were now eight and six years old, of course knew of the impending change of their routine. Both parents had spoken with them and assured them that their lives would pretty much go on as normal, and that they would both get an opportunity to spend time with mom and dad individually.

"What about Christmas?" Michael asked his dad one day.

"Well, you will probably spend that day around the Christmas tree in the West Side apartment, but I will certainly see you during the holidays, and I will have Christmas presents for both you and Rose Marie."

As predicted, the financial settlement was jarring for Graham. Linda would get 50% of all his assets. It was a sizeable sum. Quite honestly, Graham didn't know he had that much money. In addition, he would contribute a substantial amount of help for their high school and college tuitions.

All in all, it had been a five-month process of negotiations between Linda and Graham's lawyers. And then in one day, it was all over.

The mayor had kept his p.r. pro, Linda Quinlan, apprised of the proceedings. According to her, she would try to minimize all publicity on this matter. Prior to the verdict, there was absolutely no publicity. However, now that it was a done deal, she would need to issue a press release.

It was terse. The main points were divorce by mutual consent, and shared custody of the children. There was no mention of money (and if asked, she would say that is private between both parties).

Within the next few days, there were a few blurbs in the NYC newspapers. Mostly just a paragraph or two. Nothing explosive. Nothing incriminating.

Within a week, the coverage faded and it became a non-story. Perhaps that's the reality of current times, when almost one out of every two marriages end in divorce,

20

Readjustment

Mayor Kruse found it difficult to get back in the swing of things after his divorce.

On his first weekend with the kids he took them to Jones Beach on Saturday, where they enjoyed milkshakes, lots of cookies, an early dinner…and then a movie.

On Sunday, he treated them a Circle Line boat cruise around Manhattan, and then a visit to South Street Seaport, where they ended up having a casual meal overlooking the water. By 7:30 p.m., he brought them back home with hugs and "I love you's" for both kids.

The hours seem to fly by, and Graham realized it would be another month before he could enjoy their company again. Yikes!

It was still too soon in his second term to start a completely new project. Fortunately, in the next few hours, a call came which promised a delightful change of pace.

"Mayor Kruse," his secretary called out to him. "I have the British foreign secretary on the phone. His name is Sir Richard Barker. Can you speak to him right now?"

"Absolutely," Graham answered. "Let me write down his name and please connect me." When he heard the connection go through, he spoke. "Yes, sir, Mr. Barker…what can I do for you?"

The British voice answered. "I don't think we've ever met, Mayor Kruse…but I have a meeting in Washington soon, and I would love to stop by and visit with you beforehand.

"Wow, that would be great," Graham immediately responded. "When would you be coming?"

Well, I have a meeting with the President in D.C. on Friday June 12, but I could be free on that Thursday"

The mayor looked at his calendar and discovered that it would be he week after his time with the kids. "Perfect," the Graham responded. "Anything specific you want to discuss or see?"

"Well, I figure I will have a whole day of meetings in Washington with the President the next day. That will be all business. My visit to New York City is mostly to sightsee. London and New York are very similar in many ways. London has 8.6 million people. New York City has 8.5 million."

"Trying to brag?" Mayor Kruse teased him.

"Not at all," Sir Richard chuckled. "We have almost 200,000 U.S. born residents in England. I would just like to know the big city better. Make it fun. Show off the city."

"Ever been on a NY subway?" Graham asked.

"No, but I'd like to." Sir Richard responded.

"Been to Central Park?"

"I've only been to New York a few times…and it's mostly been all business," the foreign minister acknowledged.

"I'll do an itinerary for Thursday May 11, and I guarantee it will be fun. Need a place to stay?" the mayor asked.

"No thank you. I'll stay in the British consulate," the foreign minister assured him.

"Well, I look forward to it," the mayor said.

"As do I," the Consulate General agreed. "See you soon."

Graham heaved a big sigh of relief. That call made his day. It would give him a good project for the next few weeks. He knew it would be fun to be a tour guide for his favorite city.

He envisioned that there would be opportunities for a few quick speeches between the Consulate General and himself. It would also provide easy p.r. possibilities.

Immediately, he called Liz Quinlan to pick her brain about picturesque and interesting sites. "Just one day," the mayor advised. "And as the foreign minister requested, "Make it fun."

21

Commencement Time

Mayor Kruse was determined to stay out of trouble, at least for the time being. However, he did not want to start brand new projects right now. Too much going on with his family needs.

A good stopgap at this time of year would be delivering commencement addresses at some of New York's amazing colleges and universities. It would help him connect with a young audience, and their parents. It would help position him as a visionary. And inevitably, it would generate good press.

His first foray was at Columbia University, one of the most prestigious colleges in the country, dating from the 18th century (in 1784 it was renamed Columbia from its previous moniker, King's College). To this day, it is consistently listed as one of the five best college in the entire United States.

More than a thousand students were in their caps and gowns (along with their parents) waiting for the commencement address to begin.

When the mayor approached the podium, he gave thumbs up to the entire crowd.

"You should be very proud of yourselves. This is not an easy school, and that's what makes it all the more impressive that you are ready to graduate with flying colors.

"It will stand you in good stead for the rest of your lives. I am asking you to do something impressive. Something that will enrich your community. Give back. Help those who need help. Its actually in the modern DNA of Columbia.

"Many people think if this place an elitist school. A place for people of privilege. And yeah, it is expensive. But those of you who have attended this fine institution know it is a very egalitarian school. The fact is, 52% of all students here identify themselves as persons of color."

He had at least 20 minutes of other compliments for Columbia, but it was the racial diversity story that captured the media's attention.

At NYU, his message was quite different. For one thing, it is one of the largest private universities in the U.S--with more than 40,000 students. Located in Washington Square, it is also the college closest to City Hall.

As the mayor gave his commencement here, what impressed him most was the school motto: To persevere is to excel. It became the theme of his address.

"In this thrill-a-minute world, I want to encourage you to have patience. Perhaps you will be an instant success, but it may take years. Stick with it. Don't despair. Remind yourself that Richard Branson didn't make it big until he was in his forties. Think of Walt Disney shooting to fame even later in life. Consider that Ted Turner didn't start CNN until he was in his 50's. Be patient. It's a long life. And the best may come in middle age."

His surprise commencement choice was at the American Musical and Dramatic Academy—a two-year junior college located in downtown Manhattan.

For those who know the mayor, it is not surprising that he wanted to include such an institution. For the longest time, has believed one of the greatest attributes of New York City is its embrace of the arts.

In his address to the graduating class, he drove home that theme.

"Is your degree worth any less than one that involves physics or chemistry? In my book, no. Is it any less noble than a degree in medicine? Again, in my opinion, no. Should you have studied math or law or engineering or genetics or architecture? I, for one, am happy you studied how to make music. How to make people smile. How to make people feel. In my opinion, there is no higher mission...and it's one thing that separates NYC from all other metropolitan areas, perhaps all over the world.

"You are to be congratulated. You are to be applauded. (the mayor then put his hands together and applauded the graduates). Hopefully, you will earn more applause like that throughout your lifetime.

"I wish you a lifetime of smiles and satisfaction. And I thank you for living up to the unique heritage of the Big Apple."

At the end of his speech here there was applause—both from the students and their parents. There were also good review in all the newspapers for all three addresses. The mayor was pleased with his delivery and his points, and actually inspired about the future of the students and his fair city.

22

The Tour Guide

Over his next weekend with the kids, he treated them to a Yankee game, where the mayor was honored to throw out the first pitch. The seats were obviously great, right behind the third base dugout, and the kids were so tickled to see their dad on the mound. "I'm so glad to see you threw it right to the catcher without bouncing the ball in the dirt," Michael complimented him.

"I'm glad, too," Graham admitted.

Rose Marie asked if dad could play catch with her sometime.

"Sure," he gleefully responded.

On Sunday, they all went to the zoo, saw the pandas and buffaloes, end enjoyed cotton candy before an outdoor lunch. Another great day!

Graham truly enjoyed these outings, and wished he had done them more frequently when he was married and in the house. Oh, well…at least, he had them now while the kids were young.

A few days later, the foreign minister of the U.K. visited the mayor in New York City. Graham had a full agenda for their Thursday together.

It started around 8:30 in the morning at Gracie Mansion. The mayor had invited Sir Richard to share some coffee or tea before embarking on a sightseeing day.

Thanks to his research, the mayor had learned that the cities were in fact similar, with some significant differences. Renting an apartment is cheaper in the U.K. London had more restaurants and pubs, but they locked the doors at 11 p.m. vs. the 4 a.m. closings in New York. The Big Apple has far more convenience stores, and many are open all night. The black taxis of London are generally rated higher than the cabs of New York. Central Park was bigger than Hyde Park, and on and on.

Both cities had their share of attractions, and the men would see many of them today. "I am anxious to see so much today," the foreign minister said.

"We can leave as soon as you finish your tea," the mayor smiled.

Instinctively, both men enjoyed each other's company. They had a similar sense of humor, and a great sense of adventure.

Their first stop was Times Square, where they explored the theatre district and some outdoor restaurants, where they each had a bagel.

As scheduled, the two men had a short press conference near that park where the TKTS booth is located.

"I'm so happy to visit my new friend, Mayor Kruse."

"What brings you to New York?" one reporter asked.

"The bagels," Sir Jim answered. "They are hard to find in London…especially with (a pause as he thought of the word)…smere?

"Schmear," the mayor corrected him.

"Schmear," the foreign minister repeated.

That was the tone and manner of the day. It was easy and relaxed. Their next step on the agenda: a trip on the subway. As the mayor admitted from his research, the Tube is easier to navigate, but the subway cars are bigger and air-conditioned.

"Nice,' Sir James acknowledged.

The subway brought them downtown, and the two men walked a few blocks to the 9/11 memorial.

Sir James found it emotionally moving and quite dramatic. As he told the press, "the entire world wept when those planes crashed into the twin towers, but it seems that New York City has an uncanny knack for bouncing back."

After his short speech, there was a nice round of applause from the press.

Their next stop? The top of the Empire State building. Thanks to advance planning, the two men had priority access on the elevator.

"What a beautiful view," Sir James "Wow, you can see the whole city!"

From there, they went to Rockefeller Center, then Central Park, where they enjoyed a carriage ride. Then South Street Seaport, where they enjoyed an outdoor cocktail at the end of the day.

The foreign minister had thoroughly enjoyed his time with the mayor, but also felt he should call it a day so as to prepare for his meeting with the President tomorrow.

"You're a good guy," Sir James said.

"Sometimes," Graham admitted.

"Well, you were amazing today. If we lived in the same city, I think we could be best friends."

"That would be nice," the mayor admitted.

"Oh, and by the way, you should consider coming to London and visiting me. Consider this my invitation."

"Wow, that would be great." Graham honestly answered.

"You should think of becoming secretary of state or the foreign service after your tenure as mayor."

"Oh, god knows what the future will hold." Graham said.

"Do you know the President?'

"As a matter of fact, I do. When he was secretary of state, he often flew through New York and we would sometimes get together."

"I am going to tell him I am impressed with you. He's not as fun as you are, but he is a good man.

"Agreed," Graham added.

In a few minutes, the two men had their last presser of the day.

The mayor introduced Sir James, and told the crowd what a delightful day they had.

Then the foreign minister spoke.

"Our two cities have so much in common, but not surprisingly, I know London so much better. That's why I was so pleased when your wonderful mayor offered to show me some of the sights. It's a beautiful place, full of energy and creativity…and yes, busy, busy business.

"I am particularly grateful to get to know your mayor much better. What a great bloke he is. You folks are lucky to have such a wonderful advocate of the city.

"As I told him earlier, we could be best friends. As a matter of fact, we probably already are.

"Anyway, enjoy your wonderful city this weekend. And come visit us in London some day."

There was a nice round of applause for the two men. As expected, there were some good photos of the duo and positive stories in the press.

23

Childcare

As Graham fully understood, it was time to get back to the real job of governing New York City.

He had charged two deputy mayors to study and make recommendations for better NYC childcare. One was the deputy mayor of Education. Her name was Katie Hobbs. The other was the deputy mayor of the budget. Her name was Caroline Edwards.

Both women agreed that better childcare would be a godsend, especially for single mothers and lower wage families.

Katie Hobbs spoke first and underscored that the priority should be pre-K. "We have plenty of excellent grade schools, and the curriculums are quite well-respected. In fact, we are rated as one of the best systems in the country."

"That's good to hear," the mayor nodded.

"The problem is before grade school begins. There are a few facilities for this around town, but they are not really part of our public school system, and they are quite expensive...so unless you are a rich parent, they are often out of reach.

"In addition...we may be able to set up more Pre-K schools, but most working moms need childcare too in the afternoon, so that just adds to the cost."

"What's a typical bill?" Graham asked.

"At least 10 grand. I would say it could easily get to 20, 000 grand a year."

"Yikes," the mayor instinctively responded.

The mayor turned to his deputy for the budget. "Any financial relief we could offer?" he innocently asked.

"Well, if the pre-K is part of our school system, we could probably offer a break… but it's the childcare afterwards that bumps up the price, and that's not part of the public school system."

"Who uses childcare," Graham wondered out loud.

"Any woman that works. If it's a professional woman, perhaps one who is part of a successful marriage, it's probably doable. But here's the rub—there are a lot of single moms out there. And many of them make less than generous salaries."

The mayor asked her to run some numbers. "Can you figure out a cut off point…one that would signify "the haves" and "have nots" on this subject?"

"Sure," Caroline answered. "It will probably take a little guesswork on my part…but I'll do my best to keep it fair."

"That's good. Well, let's see where it leads," the mayor said and concluded this meeting.

* * * *

They met again in two days. By then, Caroline had a better idea of what income would be most hurt by pre-K and childcare.

"I think $70,000 is the line of demarcation," she suggested. "Given the costs of living in New York City—food, housing, transportation, taxes—It's tough. If you make less than that, it's hard to justify sending your kid to Pre-K and childcare."

"I see," Graham let it sink in. "Question: what if we offered a city-wide tax break for any single mother making less than $70,000? In other words, if they want to send their kid to pre-K and childcare… it would cost them nothing. The city would pay for that if they made less than $70,000. How would that sit?"

Caroline answered, "I think you would be called a hero by every single mother in New York City."

Katie smiled and agreed. "That would give every young kid in New York City a head start in life. Parents would thank you. So would pre-K teachers."

"Let's move forward in that direction then," Graham nodded. Caroline, work out the numbers, what would this cost the city. And Katie, figure out a curriculum and activities that I could sell to the public.

Both deputy mayors agreed, and locked arms on their way out of the mayor's office.

Once they left, Graham looked out the window and couldn't help but exude a proud smile. It felt good to get back to real work. It was nice solving problems for the citizens of New York, especially when he instinctively believed it would be good for everyone involved.

24

Out of the blue

The call was completely unexpected.

"Mr. Mayor, I have a Sarah Roberts on the phone from Daily Mail newspaper in the U.K. She would like a word with you."

"Put her on, "Graham said, figuring it was simply a follow up on his day with the foreign minister. "Hello, Ms. Roberts?"

"You can call me Sarah," she answered in a husky voice.

"Sarah, what's on your mind?"

"I saw some of that visit with you and Sir James Barker. I know him well, and I have to admit I don't think I ever saw him in a better mood. You must be quite a charmer."

"Maybe just one of those lucky days, "Graham answered.

"Wow, humble too," the woman responded. After a moment, she continued.

"I got thinking, I could use one of those "better mood" days. I'm only in New York for a night, but I wondered if you would like to join me for a cocktail."

"Well, that's the best offer I have had in months," Graham answered. "Where are you?"

"I'm in a townhouse of a friend, who is out of town. It's quiet here…and to be honest, it's a little lonely. I just thought, seeing the magic that you worked on Sir James the sourpuss, it might be worth a try." After a pause, she added, "Join me for a cocktail?"

"Sounds like a damn good idea," Graham answered, took down the address, and told her he would be there within an hour.

As he told himself, if she looks like a dog, it can be one drink and goodbye. On the other hand, hey.. what do I have to lose? Just to prepare his eyes for the visit, he looked her up on Google and the Daily Mail website. "Omigod," the involuntarily exclaimed. "She looks a little like Scarlett Johansson!"

Instinctively, he put on a fresh tie and doused his face with aftershave. Then he called his limo and directed the driver to drop him off at 255 East 89th. It looked like a well-maintained townhouse on a quiet street. When he exited the car, he told the driver that he needn't wait. "After my meeting, I'll get a taxi back to Gracie Mansion."

Graham walked up the outdoor stairwell and rang to doorbell. Within seconds, Sarah took his hand and invited him in.

"Wow, isn't this a surprise," the mayor said.

"What, the interior decorating? Or the woman?" she teased.

"Is there any interior decorating in here?" Graham parried.

"Yep, I knew it. You are a very clever boy," she grinned. "White wine?"

"That would be divine, as you Brits like to say."

"Devine, it will be," she agreed. She then toasted him and accompanied it with a hug and a kiss on the lips.

He responded in kind, and even gave her a French kiss. "Are you always so forward?" he wondered out loud.

"Only with people who I instinctively think are good for me,"

"And you think I am good for you?"

So far, yes," she answered and then started rubbing his crotch.

Before long, they were in the back bedroom completely disrobed. Within 30 minutes, the couple enjoyed a memorable orgasm. It was the first of several that evening.

Unfortunately, by 7 a.m., Sarah rubbed his back and said she had to get ready for a flight home to London.

"Aw damn," he uttered.

"Well, you probably have to get to work too," she offered.

"True."

Graham asked her how often she came to New York.

"Only once or twice a year," she admitted.

"Shit. This was fun. Hoped we might be able to do it again sometime.

After a pause, she said, "Come to London some time and look me up."

"I might just do that," he responded, reminded by Sir James' invitation.

Until then…." He then give her a long passionate goodbye kiss and walked outside.

Within minutes, he was able to hail a taxi back to Gracie Mansion.

All through the ride, he kept recollecting every minute of the evening. He hoped he would be able to clear his mind enough for a day's work, but quite frankly he doubted it.

* * * *

A week later, he received a postcard from her. It simply said, "Nice to meet you in New York. Sarah."

"Wow, discreet too," the mayor believed. He then vowed to visit London sometime in the next year. No rush needed. He had work to do in the months ahead. But in his heart, he knew it would be a good idea and a beautiful time.

25

Back to business

The mayor was quite dedicated to making his two big priorities come true in the months that still remained in his second term.

Trying to have the police force mirror the community seemed to be off to a good start. According to Andrew, his deputy mayor for criminal justice, there had in fact been an attrition of older white cops in the past few months. (NYC offered them a tax-free year of float if they had reached 59 and wanted to retire a year early). It had created an opening for over 1,000 new hires.

The minority targeted recruitment ads had evidently been successful. The Black recruitment ad had attracted 4000 new applications in the past six months.

The Latino ad had just broken a few weeks ago, and both Graham, Andrew, and Liz anticipated it would be equally successful.

It went like this:

Latino cops: La occupacion est beuno.
You get to keep your amigos safe.
You keep the traffic moving.
Monfeuer est traffic moviendo
Gracias. El delito est menor.
White cop: And we need you.
Latino cop: Tendra a mucho respeto
White cop: Why not apply?
Latino cop: It could be the most important job you will ever have.

Once again, everyone in the spot is wearing a police uniform. At the end there is NYPD logo, a phone number and an email address.

Graham and Andrew anticipated sending applicants to fill openings, ideally in precincts that had a large Hispanic population.

As relates to the pre-school and childcare initiative, Katie Hobbs, the deputy mayor for education talked to many primary schools to see if they could accept younger students. She also recruited lots of community buildings to see if they could be converted to childcare centers.

However, it was Mayor Kruse who energized the effort. He visited many of the lower income neighborhoods of New York City, and explained that he wanted to make pre-school and childcare more affordable to moms who were financially stretched.

In many of these forums, friendly press covered the event and the proposal that those who made less than $70,000 a year should get a break. And their kids should be given an equal opportunity in New York City.

It gathered steam, and became a reality within the next 12 months.

26

The President is Calling

When Graham's secretary told him that President Garvey was on the phone, he shoved aside everything he was currently working on and became very attentive.

"I think we have met," the President said.

"Yes sir, we have. When you were Secretary of State before your recent election, you would occasionally fly through New York City on the way to everywhere, and we got together a few times."

"Yes, l do recall." President Garvey said. "Occasionally, a flight would be hopeless delayed and you were always kind enough to say, I'll come to JFK and help with anything you need."

"What can I do for you sir," the mayor asked.

"Not much right now," the President answered. This is a belated call, but I just wanted to thank you for showing the foreign secretary of the U.K. such a great time when he stopped by NYC a few months ago, before his trip to Washington D.C."

"It was my pleasure," Graham answered. "Actually, we got along great. I basically functioned as his tour guide for New York City for one day. We had some good laughs, and even a few bagels."

"So I heard. He was very impressed with you."

"Well, the feeling was mutual," the mayor honestly admitted.

"Sir James told me he was going to invite you to visit him in London."

"He has done so. It's an open invitation, but I've been a little busy with work in New York City."

"Only for another year. You know you can only run for two consecutive terms as mayor."

"Yes, I have been told that."

"Do you have any idea what you might want to do next?"

"Quite honestly, I haven't thought of it yet," Graham answered. "I'm just trying to do a bang-up job right now for the citizens of New York."

"Right," the President agreed. "But when your term is done, I can always use good people in the federal government...especially ones that seem to instantly hit it off with foreign leaders."

"Wow," you've given me something to think about," the mayor blushed and nodded.

"Why don't you think about taking that trip to London and seeing the foreign secretary. Make it just a few day trip, and see if you can deal with the jet lag. It's a little premature on my part, but I can always use good people in the foreign service.

I am absolutely Sir James would be delighted to see you for one day, and you can always find things to do in London."

"I may take you up on your offer," the mayor acknowledged.

"Check your schedule. Give him a call. See if you can set aside a day at the consulate general's office to talk about shared interests. I can send you some notes about what our priorities are with the U.K. at the present time. There is no need to negotiate with Sir James. I just want you to be armed with what we are thinking about here in Washington, D.C.

"After a day of it, you can be on your own. See a play. Go to Harrods. Enjoy a soccer game. Whatever."

"Wow, that sounds like a great trip. Thanks for suggesting it," the mayor said.

"And when you get back, I'd love to touch base with you and figure out if the foreign travel agreed with you.

"Yes. Yes. Yes. Just so you know sir, I have travelled a bit in my younger days...and I seemed to adapt well to the change of times and seasons.

"That's great to hear," the President responded. "Keep in touch and good luck."

The next day, Graham asked his secretary to contact Sir James Barker in the U.K. On the phone, Sir James was delighted to hear from his friend in NYC. "Of course, I meant it," the foreign minister said. "I would love to visit with you an entire day here in London."

Together, they agreed upon a date about a month from now. Graham made sure it wouldn't interfere with any of his weekends with the kids.

When he finished the call to Sir James, he did retrieve the postcard from Sarah of the Daily Mail. Perhaps if things worked out, they could have another glass or two of white wine, or more.

27

On the road

Graham had another great weekend with the kids. On Saturday, he treated them to a day at Coney Island in Brooklyn. The hit of the day was of course, the Cyclone roller coaster. Yes, it's a little scary for little ones…but they both wanted to go on it again. Other attractions that interested the family were the Mermaid Parade, the circus sideshow, and a meal at Nation's Famous, where the hot dog eating contest happens every year.

On Sunday, the family took the Circle Line boat cruise around all of Manhattan. It happened to be a bright clear day, which makes the trip particularly beautiful. After a meal at a nearby waterfront restaurant, the mayor brought his kids back to their Upper West Side home, and sadly said goodbye again.

It was a few days before the mayor would embark on his trip to London to visit with his new friend, Sir James Barker, the foreign secretary of the country.

In view of the fact that the President of the U.S. had encouraged the trip, Graham decided to stay in a place called The White House hotel (no connection to 1600 Pennsylvania Avenue). Actually, it was located at 102 Sussex Garden in the London city center. The place was very clean with a 24-hour front desk and a free continental breakfast, but other than that, nothing fancy.

The mayor had taken the overnight flight, and slept several hours in an airplane seat, but looked forward to a few hours of shut-eye in the a.m. In the afternoon, he took a 9-minute walk to Hyde

Park, where he particularly enjoyed Speaker's corner. After that, a 14-minute walk to the Marble Arches.

Then he checked back home to see if anything was happening in the U.S.

"All clear," his secretary said. "Enjoy your stay. If anything comes up, which I doubt since I have cleared your calendar, I will call you."

Afterwards, he placed a call to Sir James to make sure that they were on at 9 a.m. the next morning. The foreign secretary suggested two days together because, according to him, he had a good surprise in store for Thursday afternoon. Also, on Wednesday afternoon, I wonder if you would be so kind as to address my staff at the end of the day, perhaps just a half hour hello, followed by cocktails. I think they would love to meet you."

"Sounds good," the mayor answered.

After that, a quick call to Sarah, the sexy newswoman from the Daily Mail. She agreed that Friday afternoon would be a good time get together again, and gave him her address.

As Graham had to admit to himself, it promised to be a fun, exciting memorable trip.

28

Day One in London

Graham arrived ten minutes before 9 a.m. at 1 Carlton Gardens in Whitehall, the office of Sir James Barker, the foreign secretary for all the U.K. It was one of those historic, multi-story white stone buildings that you often see in London.

When he told the receptionist his identity and his appointment, she said, "Yes, he's expecting you. Come with me to the elevator. It's on the third floor

He followed her to the elevator, hit the 3 button, and was greeted by a secretary, who invited the mayor to follow her to Sir James' office. When Graham entered, the foreign secretary was leaning on his desk, and immediately gushed, "Ah, my new best friend. Welcome to New York east."

"I do see some similarities," Graham said.

"There are some, but there are also many differences."

"I'll bet." The foreign secretary then spoke to his secretary. "Stephanie, how about a few cups of tea? Or Graham, would you prefer coffee?"

"Actually, yes…I would."

"See!" Sir James responded. "There are differences."

The NYC mayor filled in the foreign secretary on his recent activities and thanked him for the recent compliments shared with the President.

"I'll bet you'll earn many more after this trip," Sir James said, and then explained his proposed itinerary for day. I say we start at the Tate Museum, since I know you like modern art. Maybe a boat cruise? If you are game, I think it would be fun to visit the home of the Beatles and walk Abbey Road. Kew Gardens. Covent Garden. Let's play it by ear in the afternoon. As I mentioned on the phone, I would like to introduce you to our staff at 4 p.m. If you care to say just a few words, I'm sure they would appreciate it."

"I would be glad to." Graham said, rubbing his hands together. "Let's get started."

Graham very much enjoyed the Tate Modern Museum. For starters, he loved the location—bankside from the Thames. Not surprisingly, he loved the art, which showcases masterpieces from all over the world.

After that, the two men proceeded to Black Friar's Pier. Here, they boarded a high-speed boat for trip through London on the Thames. Unlike most customers who were dressed casually, the two politicos looked out of place in their suits and ties. But as Graham said, "Who gives a shit?" They put on life jackets and took their seats. Unlike the Circle Line in New York City, this experience is exhilarating and breathtaking. It races past Shakespeare's Globe, the Tower of London and Canary Wharf.

When the power boat came to a rest 45 minutes later, Graham asked Sir James, "Have you ever been on this?"he responded.

Next stop: Covent Gardens where the two guys watched street performers (very creative pantomime mostly, some musicians and tap dancers). Afterwards, they strolled through some of the streets featuring shops, and visited Neil's Yard, where they found a nice place to enjoy a cup of tea and lunch. "Oh, that's right," Sir James remarked. "You prefer coffee."

"I think in view of the occasion, I should try the tea," he chuckled.

Over two delicious chicken salad sandwiches, both men discussed ways that the U.K and the U.S. could be even closer.

"The arts may be a good start," the foreign secretary wondered out loud. "Maybe we could encourage our artists to show more work in your museums and vice-versa."

"That should be easy to arrange at the Tate and MoMA," the mayor agreed. Then he added, "Trade seems to be a burning issue all over the world."

"True, but scientifically and technology-wise, our two cultures are pretty equal."

"Yes, so maybe some other kind of give-and-take."

"Perhaps we could offer a more liberal exchange policy for college students, the mayor suggested.

"I love that idea," Sir James nodded. I'll figure out what kind of financial incentive it may take."

"I will too," the mayor agreed.

After lunch, the two leaders enjoyed a respite from the world's current problems. They visited the home and museum of the Beatles. Graham enjoyed seeing the many images of John, Paul, George and Ringo. He even bought a few LP's in one of the stores. Afterwards, the two leaders walked across the white striped walkway on Abbey road. Both men couldn't resist asking spectators to take cellphone photos of them Beatles-style.

Then they visited Kew Gardens and the botanical museum, where they viewed every exotic plant imaginable. Afterwards, the foreign secretary looked at his watch, and announced that they should get back to the consulate for the 4 p.m. meeting with his staff.

"Let's go," Graham agreed.

The foreign secretary whisked them back to Whitehall, and the two leaders took the elevator to the third floor. Instead of going straight to Sir James' office, he escorted the mayor to a meeting room filled with people.

Graham had only anticipated a few dozen people. Instead, there were probably 150 men and woman who were evidently on staff.

Sir James held up his hands and welcomed the crowd.

"I'd like to introduce an excellent ally of the U.K, and a good friend. His name is Graham Kruse and he is the mayor of New York City. We met a few months ago, and I was immediately impressed—both with what we have in common, and what kind of future we may have together, both as people and as countries. Please welcome the honorable Graham Kruse, mayor of New York City."

Graham went to the front of the room and cleared his throat. "Wow, I didn't expect a crowd this large, but I assume you get together like this every Wednesday afternoon around this time for glass of wine together."

There was some laughter from the group of people.

"As I told your boss when he was in New York, our cultures have so much in common. Not every place does, as I am sure you have discovered in the foreign service. There are places that want to oppose progress. There are places that are outright enemies. There are places that wake up angry, and want that to be tone of the day.

"We must resist this. Not with guns or bombs, but with diplomacy. Fortunately, you are not alone. There are many countries that are in your corner and share your values. Chief among them is the United States of America.

"As your boss and I learned in New York and today as we walked through London, it feels good to have friends. Let us raise a glass and wish that this friendship can only get stronger in the next few hundreds of years.

"With an ally like the U.K. I look forward to that."

Sir James continued the toast. "To us. The U.K. The U.S. and you...who help bring us both together."

There was applause and the clinking of glasses.

Sir James immediately approached the mayor and clinked his glass. "That was amazing. Impromptu. Meaningful. You are good."

"Well, I got through it. And it was sincere, "Graham admitted.

"I recorded it. With your permission, I would like to send it to the President.

He seems impressed with you, and this will only make it more so."

"Suit yourself," the mayor said.

"OK, I shouldn't monopolize you. I am sure some of the staff would like to say hi. Go circulate. Enjoy yourself....but I want to touch base with you before you go."

"OK," Graham nodded.

Over the next half hour, the mayor mingled with many dozens of the British diplomats. Everyone complimented him on his address. All agreed that the U.K and the U.S. were amazing allies.

When the crowd started to thin, Graham sought out Sir James. "You wanted to speak to me before the end of the meeting?"

"Yes, he motioned to the server to fill his wine glass again, and the mayor's too. "Cheers. Nice job again."

"Thanks."

After a sip, the foreign secretary invited Graham to follow him to his office.

He showed him to an armchair and took the other one to its left. "I told you over the phone that I might have a surprise for you on this visit."

"Yes, you did," Graham agreed.

Without further ado, Sir James spoke. "The Queen would like to visit with us tomorrow afternoon."

"The Queen?'

"The Queen."

"Omigod."

The foreign secretary paused and then continue. "She has heard good things about you, and I think just wants to get to know you better."

"Who would be in the meeting?" the mayor asked.

"Just me, you, and Queen Elizabeth II."

After a sip of his wine, Graham shook his head in disbelief. "How long would the meeting last?"

"Typically, when I have had similar meetings with the Queen and chiefs of state, 30 to 45 minutes is usually the limit.

"Omigod," the mayor just repeated again.

"However, there will usually be an after-meeting," the foreign secretary said. A roomful of press people will want to see you and the Queen together and get some pictures. If you have something to say at that time, that's usually ideal. It doesn't have to be any longer than your address you just gave to my staff of diplomats."

"So what do you have in mind for tonight? You have plans?" the foreign secretary asked.

"I do now," the mayor said. "I want to do a little research on my computer about the Queen's issues in case they come up. But I will see you tomorrow again at 9 a.m."

"That's great. We'll do a few things during the day to take your mind off of things."

"O.K." Graham said, and shook hands. "Thanks for a wonderful day."

"See you tomorrow," Sir James said and waved goodbye.

29

The Queen's Day

In the mayor's mind, all the sightseeing attractions before his afternoon meeting with the Queen amounted to nothing more than foreplay. Even so, he did his best to enjoy every one. After all, maybe the Queen would want to quiz him on them.

His first stop with Sir James was at the Tower of London. Amazingly, he learned that it was 900 years old, and had a very uneven history. Despite the beauty of the building, it has housed many famous and infamous prisoners throughout the years. Germane to his afternoon royal meeting, he also discovered that it houses many of the crown jewels to this day (some of which the Queen still wears). As he looked at them, it was quite easy to imagine them adorning the Queen, particularly the colorful crowns.

For a change of pace, the two men then visited the London Eye, that big Ferris wheel which is impossible to miss in the London sky. As he discovered talking to the staff there, it is still the most popular tourist attraction, attracting 3 million visitors annually.

During the noon hour, Sir James treated the mayor to a lunch at the Hard Rock Café in Piccadilly Circus. Over omelets, the foreign minister tried to reassure the mayor not to fear the meeting with the Queen. "The fact is, she rarely expresses political views. She leaves that to the Prime Minister. As she often tells people that's not her job as a monarch."

"I'll try to relax," Graham answered.

They closed off the sightseeing at the British Museum, which the mayor particularly liked. One claim to fame--it is the first public national museum on the world. It captures 2 million years of human history and culture—not just from the U.K., but also from ancient Greece, Rome, and Egypt. In addition to all the historic displays, it also has a great selection of games and puzzles in the shop. Graham was tempted to buy a few souvenirs, but decided it would be awkward to bring them to his Royal summit.

At 3:30, the foreign minister's driver delivered the two men to Windsor Castle. Graham stood outside the impressive structure and took a deep breath before entering the building.

"Come with me" the foreign secretary urged. "I know the way."

At the front gate, he showed his I.D. and assured security that the man at his side was an invited guest. Even so, the man at the front of the building wanted to see I.D. from Graham and asked him to sign in.

Within a few minutes they walked up a few elegant stairs and waited in chairs outside the Queen's office. Through an open door, they could see her going through some paperwork. At exactly 4:00 p.m., Sir James knocked on the door and announced that her visitor was with him.

She waved them to come in.

As he had learned on the computer last night, Graham did a small bow and said, "Your majesty, it is an honor to meet you."

"And it's nice to meet you, Mr. Mayor. I have heard such wonderful things about you from Mr. James Barker."

"That's very nice of him, ma'am." He had learned from the computer that after the first "your majesty," she should simply be addressed as "ma'am."

"What brings you to London?" she innocently asked.

Well, that was a lay-up. "I met your foreign secretary on a trip to New York City, and we had I would say an instantly simpatico relationship. He invited me to London to learn more about our similarities."

"Yes, and what have you discovered?" the Queen asked.

"Many things. These two cities have a lot in common, as I am sure you know from your many travels to the U.S."

"I've been many times," she said.

"Yes, and I for one wish to thank you for your addresses to the U.N. and the fact that you officially opened a memorial garden for British victims in the aftermath of 9/11. Perhaps his research was showing, but he was pleased to be able to show some knowledge of the monarch's influence in the U.S., and particularly New York City.

"That was an awful incident," the Queen said, reflecting on 9/11.

"Yes, ma'am. Awful," the mayor agreed. "I understand that you are the patron of 600 organizations and charities," Graham proffered.

"It's the least I can do," the Queen stated.

"Well, I very much admire that," said the mayor.

That repartee captured the tone and manner of the next 15-20 minutes. Sir James was right. She rarely ventured into dangerous politics. In a way, it was just like talking to a dear aunt or grandmother.

In a short while, her assistant entered the room and told the threesome that the press had gathered in the meeting room and would love to have a very short informal hello.

"Shall we," the Queen asked the men. "James, if you would be so kind as to introduce the mayor, that would be very nice. I don't anticipate answering any questions. I rarely do. I am there mostly to smile," she kidded the mayor and actually winked at him.

Once they entered the press room, the foreign secretary did a short intro.

We're here for an informal visit with the Queen," he began. "This man here is the mayor of New York City. I visited him in America, and was so taken with the man, that I suggested a meeting with her majesty. She too had heard great things about his honor, the mayor, that she graciously agreed. So I will turn it over to the mayor of New York City, Mr. Graham Kruse."

With that, the mayor stood up and addressed the group of 20-25 press people. "It is my sincere honor to meet your majesty on this visit to London." He then did that short bow that he had learned about from his research.

"As I told Sir James on his trip to New York, our cities are about the same size. We have similar transportation issues. We have the subway. You have the Tube, which incidentally is independently rated higher. We have our tall buildings. We share a dedication to the arts. We like our hot drinks—coffee or tea. Sometimes even with a juicy enhancement. Hey, I've even learned to like tea on this visit." (there was a little laughter from the news folks).

"So, I have spent the last few days visiting museums here. Galleries. Parks and restaurants. All good. But I thought I would tell you what I liked best about London. Perhaps this will surprise you since you all live here, and have become accustomed to it. What I like best about London is….(drumroll please) the people.

"I find your citizens incredibly friendly, even to someone like me who doesn't speak with a proper British accent. The workers here are optimistic. Even the Black Taxi drivers are courteous. And the people in the shops have a good sense of humor. (after a pause) I am charmed.

"Because I have had more interaction than in any previous trips to the U.K., I am certainly more aware of it. I love it.

"In closing, I wish to thank my new best friend Sir James Barker for squiring me around town the last few days. And I would like to thank her Majesty for meeting with me. And I would like to thank all of you for showing up this afternoon.

"Rather than turn this into a formal stiff press conference, I would be glad to greet you all individually in the next few minutes.

"Have a great evening."

There was applause.

He then waved to the crowd and started shaking hand. As he did so, the Queen waved goodbye to the mayor and walked out the room with a smile on her face.

The mayor spent several minutes introducing himself to many members of the press and answering an occasional question. For the most part they were softballs.

When he saw that Graham had a moment alone, Sir James came up to him and shook his hand. "Excellent. Nice job," he said.

"Think so?" the mayor asked.

"Absolutely. She should have seen the Queen's face. She was all smile."

"You think the ending was O.K. with no questions?" Graham asked.

"Inspired," his new buddy said. "Want to go out for a cocktail?"

"Actually, I am tired. And I just want to thank you for everything on this trip." Sir James said he understood, and waved goodbye.

As the crowd began to thin, a familiar face approached the mayor. "Hello, my name is Sarah, and I am with the Daily News. I enjoyed your address."

Of course, he recognized her and was again impressed with her discreet nature. "Well, it's nice to meet you Sarah," he said as if talking to a complete stranger.

"Here is my card, if you have any questions about London," she offered with a business like handshake. On the back, was written 6:45 p.m. tomorrow and her address.

30

Sarah

In the morning, Graham slept in and finally went to the dining room for the complimentary breakfast.

After that, he decided to get some exercise to loosen his muscles for a big evening. He found a place called Rapha Cycle Club, located behind Piccadilly Circus In Soho. It was relatively cheap—about twenty bucks an hour. The bike was comfortable and give him some fresh air and some easy sightseeing.

In the late afternoon, he did reach the office to see if everything was fine in NYC. "No problems," his secretary reported. "Everyone knows you are out until Monday. Just enjoy."

"I will try to," the mayor promised.

In the afternoon, he did go to Hyde Park and visit the Serpentine Gallery. And then he was free.

Around 6 p.m. he ordered a black cab to deliver him to Sarah's address in the Mayfair District. When he arrived at her flat, it frankly reminded him of the New York apartment where they first had a get-together.

At precisely 6:45, he rang the doorbell, and Sarah opened the door. She immediately invited him in with a passionate kiss on the lips. She then poured him a glass of white wine and clinked glasses.

"I've been looking forward to this," Graham said.

"I hope so," she responded.

"Why would I not?" he asked.

"I don't know. I thought maybe you found someone else," she said with a smile.

"There's only one you," he complimented her.

"Actually, tonight there may be more than one me. I've asked a girlfriend if she wanted to join us, unless you object."

"Wow," he thought. "What a naughty woman she is." Despite his experience, the mayor had never had a ménage a trois. But as he took a sip of his wine, he convinced himself that there's a first time for everything.

Suddenly the doorbell rang again. Sarah looked at the mayor and asked, "Should I let her in?"

"I would hate to disappoint her," he answered.

As the door opened, there stood another gorgeous woman. Unlike his Scarlett Johansson lookalike, this one was a dark-haired beauty.

"Graham, meet Rachel." He instinctively gave her a hug and a kiss on the cheek. She responded with a kiss on lips...and then offered the same sexual hello to Sarah.

For a moment, the mayor wondered what kind of night he had in front of him. "Was this supposed to be a tryst between two women? Was he intruding? Would he be comfortable if it got out of hand? Would he be uncomfortable if it went on too long?"

In anticipation of this, he motioned to Sarah to join him in the kitchen. "I may not be able to spend the whole night. Perhaps just a few hours and then maybe I should be on my way."

"Aww," she rubbed her eyes with a fake cry.

"I've got an early morning flight," he lied. "Besides, it looks like you may have company for the evening."

"Yeah, but I would like some time with all three of us," she said.

"So would I," he said. "I just wanted to give you fair warning."

"O.K. Then let's get this party going right now." With that, she clapped her hands impulsively and moved to Rachel. She immediately took off the woman's blouse.

Rachel returned the favor, and lowered Sarah's skirt.

Just to keep things equal, both women started rubbing Graham's crotch and unzipping his fly and lowering his pants.

Within ten minutes, all three were in bed completely naked. The mayor went down on Sarah. As he did so, Rachel decided to lick his asshole. For a moment, Graham was afraid he would prematurely ejaculate. Instead, he turned over and gently placed Rachel next to Sarah, both face up.

Unaccustomed to three ways, he began to penetrate Sarah. Then Rachel. Then Sarah again. Soon, he did come inside Sarah.

After that, both women began to lick each other's vaginas, as the mayor watched. Rachel was the noisier of the two, and quite frankly, Graham was afraid she was so loud that a neighbor might complain.

"Shhh," he involuntarily uttered.

Sarah reassured him that there were no neighbors to the left or right of her

"Aww," Rachel reacted. "We were just starting to have some real fun."

"There is still time for the two of you have plenty of giggles," he answered. "I just have to get on my way."

After a big heave of a sigh from both women, they relaxed on the bed for while. Thirty minutes passed and then Sarah asked Graham if he wanted to give it another go.

"I really have to leave," he answered. "As I told you earlier, I have an early flight tomorrow back to the U.S." He put on his clothes, kissed the two women goodbye, and walked out the apartment to hail a black cab back to his White House hotel.

He had always thought of himself as an adventurous soul, but he thought perhaps he met his match with these two women.

Perhaps his ego was slightly crushed that both women seemed to enjoy each other's company…perhaps more than being with him. As he considered this, he shook his head in disbelief. Maybe he was just a one-woman man. Then he chuckled to himself. "Certainly not a one woman only man," he smiled. "But certainly one woman at a time."

By 10 p.m. he entered his hotel again, and ordered a vodka on the rocks (he remembered that London pubs close at 11 p.m.) As he sipped the clear liquid, he sat there and looked down at the table. He shook his head at his behavior and knew he would not call Sarah again.

When he got back to his hotel room, he called the airline and indeed changed his reservation to early the next morning. Somehow, he wanted to get home early, and get on a more normal footing.

31

Home, Sweet Home

After his morning flight, it felt good walking into Gracie Mansion again in the early afternoon. He immediately went to his desk and shuffled through some papers. His secretary was right, and good. She had notified everyone that Graham would be gone until Monday. Consequently, he discovered that he had missed no important meetings.

Ironically, he felt an urge to call his ex-wife. It would be the first time he spoke with her since the divorce.

"Linda, this is Graham," he began. "I know this is against the rules, but I just got back from a brutal trip to London. I know it is another one of your weekends with the kids..but I miss them. And I was just wondering if you would like a one-day only reprieve. If so, I will get together with them Sunday only and not bother you with another call like this."

There was a pause. "Do you promise this is a one-time only proposition?"

"I promise. I stewed over even calling you, but I thought what the hell...maybe you would like a break."

Another pause.

"Let's do it just this once, and not tell any of our lawyers."

"Wow, you are great. If it works for you, I will pick them up at ten, and return them early, so you'll get the entire evening with them."

"I'm not sure I should break the rules that way," she rubbed her temples, deep in thought.

"I understand."

"But I did just get a call from a couple of teachers from my school who wanted to have brunch with me on Sunday. If I decided to go, I would need to hire a sitter for most of the day or stick them with neighbors….or perhaps push the brunch a few weeks until it's your turn with the kids."

"I understand," he repeated.

"Let's do it just this once, and not tell any of our lawyers," she uttered.

"Great!" he said with a broad smile in his voice.

"Where will you take them?"

"I haven't decided yet," he honestly answered. "Haven't even thought about it till I spoke with you."

"Well, the kids seem to enjoy their adventures with you."

"Thanks. Enjoy your brunch."

"Goodbye."

"Goodbye."

Ok, it was a little awkward, but Graham was very appreciative. He checked out his list of kid activities, and decided that it might be fun to visit the Intrepid Sea, and Space museum on the Hudson River. It's a former US aircraft carrier from WWII that now houses various aircraft for viewing. It has the space shuttle, the Concorde (which could go from New York to London in a little more than 3 hours), and several Sikorsky helicopters. In the Gemini Space Capsule, the kids can sit in two small padded seats and imaging they are circling the earth and visiting the moon or other planet. They were also allowed to sit in the helicopters and fantacize about rescuing people from the Hudson River or beyond.

After that, dad treated them to the top of the Rock (Rockefeller Center) where they could enjoy a 360 degree panorama of New York city 70 stories above ground level.

After a quick lunch, they all went to the Bug Carousel in the Bronx zoo. It's just like a merry go round with horses, but instead the normal equestrian theme, this one has brightly colored big bugs on poles…so you can ride around on a big mosquito, cockroach, June bug or many others. The kids loved it and tried rides on many insects.

Unfortunately, it was getting to be time to return the kids to their home. Along the way, Graham stopped at a flower stall and bought a bouquet of flowers.

When he arrived at the apartment on the Upper West Side, he gave the kids a big hug and asked them to deliver the flowers to their mom. "Bring them to her," the mayor told Michael, and just say "Dad says thanks."

"Thanks for what," his son asked.

"Just for the chance to visit with you both today," Graham responded. He then watched the kids skip towards the front door and enter the apartment. He asked his driver to hold on for a few minutes while he let the scene and the day sink in. As he told himself, it was just the tonic he needed after that wild spree in London.

32

Back in the Saddle Again

His first week back at Gracie Mansion proved to be a comfort for Graham Kruse. There seemed to be no alarming circumstances or panic situations.

Over the next few days, he invited his deputy mayors to report and discuss the progress on the priority objectives he had set for his second term.

Katie Hobbs stated that the pre-school/childcare proposal had been met with enthusiasm by mothers throughout New York City, especially if they were single mom who were not rolling in cash. The press also applauded the plan.

The situation with school districts was more vexing. "As we discussed earlier, some of them have pre-K programs…but none of them really provide childcare after the school day is done. That will take a contribution for the city government. "As educators, they admire the goal, but they just worry about dollars and cents," she added.

"Who doesn't?" the mayor wise-cracked. "And what about the feasibility of housing some of these in units beyond parochial schools?"

"Well, I have checked a few sites. I explored office spaces in mid-town East, 34th street, Madison Avenue, and around Penn Station. In some cases, they house small businesses, which occupy many floors. However, many of them have enough space for a free floor… which could be converted to pre-school and childcare facilities. It would be a godsend for the mothers of small children who worked in the building. Of course, it would cost money, but they all seemed amenable."

"That's brilliant!" the mayor gushed.

"I am also looking at community centers in Brooklyn, Queens, the Bronx and Staten Island," she stated. "I should have rough financial figures for this by the end of next week."

"That's just great. You're a good woman for the job," he complimented her. "Keep at it."

"I definitely will. I believe in this," she said, and then exited his office.

The mayor's next visit was with Andy Madden, his best friend, and deputy mayor for criminal justice.

"How goes it?" the mayor asked.

"Pretty well. That Latino police recruiting ad is getting raves in the Hispanic community. It's also attracting thousands of applicants who now believe the police would welcome them on the force."

And are we still enjoying some vacancies in many of the precincts?" Graham asked.

"Some. We could use a few more White retirees…but that will come in the next six months.

"Wow, that sounds promising," the mayor nodded.

"It is. And once we get a police force that better mirrors the local population, we can institute plans to have more neighborhood involvement in the local communities.

"You bet," Graham agreed.

After a slight pause, the mayor addressed a topic that was germane to both men.

"You know that at the end of this second term, I cannot run for a consecutive third term. I can do it after a four-year hiatus…but according to the law, I will need to take a break."

"I am aware of that," his friend acknowledged.

"So I was wondering if you have thought about what you might do after I walk out of Gracie Mansion."

"I figure I will go back to being a prosecuting attorney," Andy answered.

"I have another thought. Why don't you run for mayor?"

"Me?"

"Yeah, you. Nobody on staff or in this city knows the job better." Graham stated and meant it sincerely.

"Oh, I am not cut out to be mayor,"

"You're good. And I believe you could do an excellent job for all the citizens of New York City."

"I don't see myself cut out for such a job," Andy answered.

"Will you at least think about it?"

"I will, but I think my wife would like to see more of me than that which is conflicted with mayor responsibilities."

"Promise?"

"I promise."

Andy was an honest guy. He would think about it. But somehow Graham knew in advance where his buddy would net out. No, he would not run for mayor.

33

Konnichiwa

The following week, the President of the United States called Mayor Graham Kruse again.

"I hear you were a hit in London. I got a tape of your address to the foreign service. Very nicely handled. And I even heard from the Queen, who only has raves about you."

"That's good to hear," the mayor admitted.

"Now I wonder if you could do one more mission for the federal government."

"What's that?"

"Well, the prime minister of Japan, Yoshihide Suga, is coming to New York city next week to visit his nephew who works there. I asked him if he could possibly spare an hour or two to meet with you."

"With me?" Mayor Kruse reacted with surprise. "I don't know a word of Japanese other than "konnichiwa," meaning "Hello.""

"Well, that's a good start," the president laughed. "Actually, he will come equipped with a translator, which will be good practice for you."

Mayor Kruse shook his head in disbelief. "What are you trying to do? Turn me into a diplomat when my term ends?"

"Something like that," said President Garvey (who had been elected after President Weiss), but would give no further hints.

"O.K. What will we be discussing?" the mayor asked.

"I would like you to pick his brain about the differences in healthcare between the U.S. and Japan. Despite our comparable strengths, I get the feeling they are well ahead of us in terms of health care, hospitalization and longevity."

"I would think so," Graham agreed.

"Well, try to get a read on how they approach things. Prime Minister Suga is a wonderful guy. In my meetings with him, he has been very open."

"Are you meeting with him afterwards?"

"Actually, no. He's only in New York City one day. Then he has to head back to Tokyo."

"O.K. I will have the meeting, and discuss it with you afterwards," Graham said.

"That would be great," the President responded. "Talk to you later."

The following Tuesday, the prime minister of Japan came to the mayor's office in Gracie Mansion. They immediately shook hands.

Graham took a page from his research on the Queen, and acknowledged him with a bow. He also said "Konnichiwa."

The translator smiled. "Wow, you know Japanese!"

"Just that one word," the mayor answered.

"Well, that's why I am here," the translator stated.

"The President of the United States asked me to pick your brain on health care. We believe Japan is far ahead of us in this regard, and we would love to learn from you how you are succeeding in this regard."

The prime minister let this sink in, and began the discussion.

"First of all, it has to do with coverage. In Japan, we have had full healthcare coverage for 60 years."

"That's a long time," Graham acknowledged.

The prime minister continued. "It costs half as much as the U.S. and produces 50% better results."

"Excellent." The mayor was taking notes and launched into his next topic. "According to my figures, the U.S. ranks 26th in the world in life expectancy. We live to about 79 years old. Evidently, Japan leads the world in life expectancy at 84 years. What's your secret?"

"Exercise," the prime minister answered. "We tend to walk more, and take less taxis everywhere."

"The mayor touched his belly, and agreed. "That's good advice."

"It makes a difference," the prime minister asserted. "Only 3.7% of Japanese are overweight, compared with 38% of Americans."

The mayor also learned that Japan had generous insurance schemes as compared with our "for profit" hospitals.

In all, they discussed many topics. However, the mayor did not want to monopolize his entire day. "You are going to visit a relative in New York?" he asked.

"Yes, he lives in the financial district," the Prime minister answered.

"Well, let me not hold you." With that, the mayor stood and said, "Arigato," (thank you). He also used the third Japanese word he had learned for this meeting.

"Sayonara," he said with a bow.

The prime minister smiled and repeated the greeting in English, "Goodbye," he said and exited the room.

"Not bad," Graham told himself. Maybe he might have a knack after all in the foreign service. While it was fresh, he decided to transcribe his scribbles into notes for the president. As usual, he would add a few of his own thoughts. It would probably take a few days, but he was pleased with the meeting and looked forward to sharing his thoughts with the President.

34

What's next?

"President Garvey is on the phone," the mayor's secretary told him.

"Did you send him that thing I typed?"

"Sent it yesterday," she answered.

"I'll take the call," Graham said, and greeted, "Yes, Mr. President."

"First of all, let me tell you that Mr. Suga thought you were brilliant. He enjoyed meeting with you, sharing ideas, and very much appreciated the points you made."

"That's good to know," the mayor answered. "Did you get my summary of notes from the meeting?"

"Yep, they are great. I am impressed that you were able to hold your own with one of the most intelligent leaders in the world."

"I also have a few other points which I didn't put on paper since I didn't discuss them with the prime minister. Would you like to hear them?"

"Of course."

"Well, for one thing, we need to get more people covered with health care coverage. Obama care was a good start…but still, there are millions of people who qualify. I would suggest you make this U.S. wide. The lower-middle class people (and the middle-class people) will thank you…and vote for you the next time around."

"That's very good," the President responded. "You have a good knack for communicating with people who are not covered."

"Agreed."

"I think perhaps we should consider lowering the Medicare age. Perhaps from the 65 it now is to 62. More and more people are retiring early and they could use the help.

"The other thing is Medicaid. Maybe you could consider expanding the coverage to include more needy souls. I believe, at present, it largely goes to some low-income people, families and children, pregnant women, the elderly, and people with disabilities. That's only in some states. Some states make it more difficult to tackling complicated global problems and opportunities."

"Lots to think about," the President responded.

After a few seconds of silence, Graham asked the question that was burning in his mind. "So what job am I auditioning for?"

"On top of that, you are very clever and perceptive," President Garvey complimented him.

"Thank you."

"You still have months to go before your second term ends, and I have a few months before I get my team together for the next four years."

"I see."

"But even so, I am thinking ahead…and I have a few questions for you. Would you object working for the federal government?"

"Not at all."

"Secondly, do you have a passport?"

"Yes, I do….how do you think I got to London last month?"

"Right," the President said. "And lastly, do you like to travel?"

"I do," the mayor admitted. Not that I have an interest in being out of the country 100% of the time. But an occasional trip here, even a week there can be enriching."

"I agree," the President said.

"A few more questions for you Mr. President. If you ever decide if there is a job for me, and if you ever decide to offer one to me… would I have to move to Washington D.C.?"

"Probably not," the President answered. "But you would have to visit from time to time to meet with me, and perhaps some other cabinet-level leaders. Even so, I would anticipate that you could still live in New York City, if that locale makes you comfortable."

"Well, it does…and my young kids still live here."

"O.K." President Garvey said.

"O.K. what?" Graham responded. "What's the job?"

After a pause, the president answered the question as best he could at the present time. "I can't tell you that at this moment. I still have someone in this job, and they will need to continue for several months. Also, you will need to complete your tenure as mayor of New York City. You can't leave until your term is up."

"That's right," Graham agreed. "But don't keep me in suspense forever. Maybe the Queen will want to hire me for speeches to the press."

"This job will be better," the President assured him. "The whole world will know who you are."

"Can't wait to hear about it," the mayor said.

"I will be in touch as we get closer to your last months on the job.

"Thanks for the consideration," Graham said. And thanks for the call."

"You are very welcome. Goodbye," and with that the President hung up the phone.

35

Hello kids

Spring and summer are something of a lull time for an elected official, especially in the tail end of his last term.

Given the fact that all students will soon be out of school, a priority is making sure the parks are in good shape, and youth activities plans are set in motion. As Memorial Day approaches, it is also a time when a mayor wants to be very patriotic and honor the sacrifices of our armed services. Of course, the same Americana sentiment occurs on the 4th of July, accompanied by one of the best fireworks displays in the country.

The other thing about those particular seasons is that it's a perfect time to be with kids, or perhaps even feel like one yourself. The New York Aquarium is always a hit, as is the Statue of Liberty. For exercise, there are bike paths, mini golf at Hudson River Park, and a swimming pool at Chelsea Pier. For pure escapism and entertainment, many families enjoy watching the New York victory theatre, which features kid's programs with a touch of circus. And then there is world-class tennis at the U.S. Open in Queens. During the warmer months, Graham did most of these things with his kids, who seemed to enjoy all the colorful sights and sounds of New York City.

Perhaps the biggest political question of the season was "Who will be the next mayor?"

Not surprisingly, there was a plethora of choices. On the Democratic side, some of the candidates were:

Wally Russell, the deputy budget director.

Frank Meyer, the comptroller who knew where every penny was hidden.

Jim Wolfe, (one of the few Black candidates in the race) of the Housing Authority.

Eric Miller, the deputy mayor for communications

Sally Cunningham, who had served three terms in the U.S. House of Representatives.

Carlos Ramiriz, who served on the City Council.

Penny Herzog, the deputy mayor for health and human services.

It wasn't just Democrats who had ambitions to be elected mayor of New York City. Chief among the Republicans were:

Brandon Tituskin, from the office of Treasury.

Benjamin Katsaros, who served as commissioner of Veteran's Services.

Alec Stern, from the office of Business services.

So the dance card of candidates was full. Some of them had asked for endorsements (as did the Press), but Mayor Kruse declined. As he told the *New York Times*, "I firmly believe it should be totally in the hands of the voters. I completely trust their instinct, and do not want to interfere in their judgment."

Not surprisingly, many of the reporters wanted to know what would be next on Mayor Kruse's agenda. "Will you run for governor? Senator? Will you go back to being a prosecuting attorney?" "We hear it might be a big announcement."

Maybe even a surprise to many people?" Can't you give us a hint?"

The mayor refused to comment on these speculations. "You will find out soon enough. But for now, I still have a job to do in Gracie Mansion, and I intend to do that until my last day."

36

The President Has a Proposal

In mid-June, after Penny Herzog had won the Democratic Primary and Brandon Tituskin had scored highest with Republican voters, the general election was in full swing. Consequently, the existing mayor was almost an after-thought on the part of voters. True, they would compare his record with the new candidates, but in their hearts they knew he would soon be gone, and the city would be poised for a fresh start, at least for a four-year term.

There were articles in *New York* magazine and the *NY Times* about his accomplishments. However, it was complete guesswork on any reporter's part as to what Graham Kruse would do next.

President Garvey cleared up that mystery with a phone call to the mayor.

"I guess you have been wondering if there any room for you in the federal government."

"Well, if you remember sir, you hinted at that."

"Really," the President teased him. "Oh yeah, I do recall some veiled conversations in that regard."

After a pause, Mayor Kruse said, "OK, enough suspense. What do you have in mind?"

"It is perhaps the best job in all of government, especially for someone with your talents."

"I'm all ears," Graham said.

After a few seconds, President Garvey said, "I think you should be our ambassador to the U.N."

"Wow," the mayor reacted with some enthusiasm.

"You have a good quality of getting along with foreign people, and I believe you are an amazing advocate for the truly American point of view."

"I believe I am," Kruse responded. "Who would I report to?"

"You would report to me, and also the Secretary of State…but you would have a lot of independence on your own. It's a cabinet-level position and would entail some travel. Some of it would be for international meetings. Some would be at your discretion if you think it would help you do the job. But it is not non-stop airplane trips."

"Can you sum up the job? What are the priorities?"

"Well, the basic job is to protect and promote U.S. interests on the world stage. It's a forum for advancing peace, security and our overall well-being among 193 member states.

"What's with your current U.N. Ambassador?"

"She wants to resign in the early fall of the year, so the timing could not be more perfect."

"What's the next step?"

The President shrugged, but Graham could not see that on the phone. "Well, I need to announce the appointment with the advice and consent of the Senate. I don't anticipate a problem there. I have privately spoken with some Senators and they all rate you highly."

"Well, I will give you an initial reaction," the mayor said. "It sounds great. Something I may truly enjoy in the years ahead."

"I was hoping you would feel that way," President Garvey remarked.

After a pause, Graham asked where he would live.

"Well, here's the good news. As I hinted on the phone earlier, you would not have to move to Washington D.C. In 2019, we purchased a penthouse at 50 UN Plaza. It's even furnished."

"Amazing," the mayor instinctively reacted.

"You would need to visit the White House occasionally or with the Secretary of State. I would need to know the burning issues that might be on the agenda. I will also advise you on my point of view, so we can minimize surprises.

"Well, that just sounds great," the mayor said. "What's the timetable? When can I tell folks?"

"Maybe in a month. I want to publicly thank our existing UN ambassador for job well-done and give her a proper send off. I also need to gain approval for you in the Senate. I promise to keep you informed of my progress in these regards. I would say that by late August or September, we could have a big celebration to announce this major move. Until then, mum's the word."

"I understand, "the mayor said. "And sir, I thank you for your confidence."

"I am sure you will do a great job and be a huge asset on the world stage for the United States of America,"the President concluded.

"Thanks again." Graham repeated and hung up the phone. In a pantomime that one might only see in high school, he then extended both hands and with clenched fists, demonstrated a dramatic victory gesticulation.

37

Celebrations

Penny Herzog had won the Democratic primary for mayor, and had scheduled a huge gala celebration at the New York Public Library on 5th and 42nd. They had a reception venue there that could handle up to 300 people.

Penny was the deputy mayor of Health and Human Services for the past four years during Graham Kruse's last stanza a mayor. He had a hunch she would be good since she was quite versed on her subject matter. However, as Graham had observed, she was not a very good speaker—more of a detail-oriented beaurocrat. However, he privately shrugged, maybe that's what New Yorkers want now.

She had visited with Kruse after her victory was declared and asked his advice. "I would create a couple of big priorities for the next four years," he said. "I would appoint good people…with a good heart for this city. And I would try your best to utilize the press and TV to keep your bold agenda fresh and alive in the public eye."

"Yech," she immediately reacted. "I don't love dealing with the press. I am more of a private person. You, on the other hand, are a natural at it. I envy you for your confidence in that regard."

"Well, good luck," he said and wished it sincerely for her.

"Will you come to my celebration and say a few words?"

"If you'd like me to," he assented.

"I very much would," she answered.

At the Public Library space, the drinks started to pour at 7:30 p.m. As Graham had promised, he would say a few words at 9 o'clock. At that precise hour, Graham clinked his glass, approached the mike, and began speaking to the crowd of about 200 people. "I would like to congratulate Penny Herzog for her fantastic victory. Or perhaps I should now call her mayor-elect Herzog. I have seen her in action during my last 4 year term, and I am pleased to tell you all that she in impressive—big ideas and the ability to bring them to fruition."

"Her specialties—health and human services—will be excellent attributes in this great city. I have found it to be the most human of all cities I have visited, and god knows, we could all be a little healthier. So I hope you listen to her and follow her in the days ahead. You will not be disappointed. She's a star, and a great advantage for the millions of New Yorkers."

He then looked at Penny and said, "mayor-elect Herzog, would you like to say

"First of all, Andy, good luck going back to the law firm. I hope it makes you happy and brings satisfaction. I also want to thank you for all you have done on behalf of me and this city."

He then turned to Liz. "Liz, my dear friend. What are you going to do in the days ahead?"

"I will probably return to my p.r. firm. They say they miss me," she joked. a few words?"

She approached the mike. "Just a few," she said. "Let's all enjoy ourselves this evening."

"Wow," Graham told himself. "Nope, she does not like to talk in front of the press or even regular people."

A few hours later, Graham encountered Andrew Madden, his friend and deputy mayor under his tenure. He also saw Liz Quinlan, his favorite p.r. woman who always made him look good.

"First of all, Andy, good luck going back to the law firm. I hope it makes you happy and brings satisfaction. I also want to thank you for all you done on behalf of me and this city."

He then turned to Liz. "Liz, my dear friend. What are you going to do in the days ahead?"

"I will probably return to my p.r. firm. They say they miss me," she joked.

"But we'll see."

"Well, I can tell you this my dear Liz." I will definitely miss you. Stay tuned about my life. I will probably participate in a major announcement in the week. But if I ever decide to run again for mayor, Liz I hope you would come again and work for me. You know me better than most people…and you know how to get the best ink for me."

Graham raised a glass and toasted both of them. He then gave them both a customary hug. With Liz, he included his familiar kiss on the cheek.

* * * *

A week later, Graham Kruse would have his big announcement at the White House. Four days ago, the President had told him that the Senate had given full approval of his appointment as the U.S. representative to the United Nations. As expected, he would meet with President Garvey and Secretary of State Daniel Davis to make sure everyone was on the same wavelength.

"I am planning a celebration and P.R. launch in the White House on this Wednesday," the President said.

"That day is good for me," Graham said.

Secretary of State Davis shook his hand. I have heard great things about you…from here, from New York, from London, from Japan. And I look forward to working with you. For the most part, I will let you have your own independence, but I will apprise you of any upcoming international issues that may affect us both. If so, we can put our heads together and come up with a game plan that benefits the United States."

"I look forward to that," Graham said.

As for the p.r. launch. The President said that he would say a few words, and then invite Graham to speak.

It was scheduled to start at 7:30 p.m. At that time, the President came to the podium and addressed the crowd."

"I am very pleased to introduce you all to our next UN Ambassador. Many of you undoubtedly know him. His name is Graham Kruse, and he has for eight years been the very successful mayor of America's largest city—New York City. During that time, he has made many improvements that benefit the U.S. and the world. In addition, he has been a great ally of our U.K friends (he even met with the Queen) and our important Japanese friends, including the prime minister.

"Ladies and Gentlemen, please welcome Graham Kruse."

After a round of applause, the new ambassador to the U.N. came to the podium. "It is an honor and privilege to serve this great nation this way," he began. "I truly love this country, and think we have much to offer the world. For one thing, we need to protect our interest. But just as importantly, we need to spread the good word about the U.S. and be an inspiration for far away places.

"I promise to do that. If it takes giving a stirring speech at the U.N., I will do so. If it takes going halfway around the planet to persuade others to see our point of view, I will also do that. In other words, whatever it takes.

"We are worth it. We are a one-of-a-kind world power. And I look forward to working with President Garvey and Secretary of State Davis to ensure that our best days are still ahead of us.

"I want to thank you all for coming, and wish you a great evening." He then saluted the crowd and mingled. There were lots of handshakes. Most of the crowd believed that it was a good hire, and wished him well.

38

New Digs

Graham moved out of Gracie Mansion two weeks before his successor, Penny Herzog would take office.

For one thing, he wanted to clear out so she would be ready roll on Day 1. In addition, his curiosity was seducing him. He wondered what that furnished penthouse at 50 U.N. Plaza looked like. He had heard that the previous U.N. ambassador had vacated the property, so he thought he would take a look.

There was no other way to describe it but magnificent. There were actually three bedrooms that were decorated as if it was out of *House Beautiful*. Each had a bed, in case either one of his kids wanted to sleep there sometime. As he viewed the elegant abode, he also couldn't help but think that it would also be a good place for a tryst.

After his recent three-way in London, he tried to reject the thought. But wait… even at the time, he was not opposed to flirts and sexuality. It had been part of his nature ever since he was in his early 20's. He just didn't want a ménage a trois. As he reminded himself. one woman at a time.

In fact, part of the appeal of this new international job was a degree of sexual and publicity safety that could come with it. Unlike an affair in the U.S. (particularly in New York City, where he could be easily identified and shamed), he hoped he could gallivant in relative privacy. In many cases, his paramours would not speak his language. Often, they might even know who he was. Consequently, it could possibly be a confidential sin. His kids wouldn't need to know. His ex-wife wouldn't need a confession. His friends wouldn't even need to who, what, where or when.

Oh, well…let's not get ahead of myself. One step at a time, and that first step was organizing his U.N. priorities and sharing them with the President and the Secretary of State.

* * * *

The next week, he called both of them and requested a meeting in Washington D.C., where he could propose an agenda that would give focus to his months ahead and offer advantages to the United States.

As he had learned in the mayor's job, unless you have such priorities, you just bounce around with the latest crisis and make it up as it goes.

As he explained to President Garvey and Secretary of State Davis, he had devised four issues which could benefit U.S.'s prestige in the world.

1. He believed global warming was an increasing priority for the U.S. and the world at large. He pointed out that hurricanes down South and forest fires on the West Coast were devastating America. Of course, many countries had it much worse. Australia for example, was losing 84 million hectares each year. China's emissions were twice the rate of America. Yes, France had started an initiative a few years back, but at the time, the U.S. did not participate. His belief? We should join with Paris and perhaps lead the way to make a mark in the world.

2. Gender equality. "Here's an area where we can show true global leadership, and gain many brownie points at home," he said. "In the Congo, 2 million women are raped each year. In Saudi Arabia women are still required to have male guardians. This is a lay-up for the United States, where we truly have a head-start."

3. Peace from rockets and warfare. Obviously, North Korea was a prime villain here. Of course, many other countries are experimenting with warfare weapons. He believed that with Japan's help, they might be able to bring a better degree of peace to the world.

4. World hunger. The number of hungry people are increasing in the world, Graham explained. In fact, one in nine people go hungry every single day. As one of the best agricultural nations in the U.N., the U.S. had plenty to gain from this initiative.

    As Graham explained, these were in no particular order. Also, he would like to pick the brains of some nations, and perhaps enlist their help with initiating global suggestion. "So what do you think," he asked the two gentlemen.

"May I speak first?" the Secretary of State asked the President, who nodded yes. "I think it's impressive, and spectacular. I will ask our diplomats for any inputs they may have on all four subjects."

The President rose from his chair and moved towards Graham. Then he shook his hand. "I had a belief you would be a real asset in this job. I now feel that my belief was 100% accurate."

"Thank you," Graham answered, and exited the room. Yes, he was off to a good start. And with some travel, it might only get better.

39

Bonjour Paris

Graham had learned that Emmanuel Macron, the prime minister of France had vowed to fight global warming. In addition, he wanted the U.S. experts to help in this battle.

Graham called the President and asked if it was O.K to just call Macron and set up a meeting. Or do you need to set it up?" he asked.

"Actually, since you have a cabinet-level position and the pedigree of a United Nations job, I think you are perfectly in order to set up such meetings by yourself,"

President Garvey said. "If you hit a snag, and I doubt you ever will, just give me a call. Also, I would love to know the outcome of your get together in Paris."

"Yes, of course," Kruse assured him.

Within a few days, he was able to contact Macron, who can speak English. Graham explained America's desire to help with global warming, particularly through the United Nations."

"That's fantastique," the prime minister said. "Come to Paris and let's talk about a path to make this happen."

Graham set up a date for next Wednesday, and asked if he could also meet with the woman who helped gain global warming signatures from nations four years ago. "I'd love to know her experience with this. What sort of resistance had she encountered.? What kind of support had she enjoyed?"

"I will gladly give you her contact number, and you can reach her directly, the prime minister said. "I'm sure she would be glad to discuss it, especially now that you are going to be more involved with the United Nations."

"Thank you," Graham said, and promised to provide his itinerary and Paris contact numbers for the Prime minister.

With his secretary's help, Kruse set up a round-trip flight.

"I hear that the Peninsula Paris is quite good," Stephanie said. A woman of about 30, she had been with diplomatic department for several years, and had a good knowledge of international destinations. "I hear they have a nice pool and great amenities," she added.

"That sounds great. Once the reservation clears, please email Emmanuel Macron my hotel, their phone number and my personal cellphone contact number."

"Of course, she responded.

* * * *

Within a week, Graham landed at Charles de Galle airport. To his pleasant surprise, it was a first class ticket. Equally pleasing, he found his hotel quite comfortable. The room was big. The food was good. The pool was warm and beautiful.

After a swim, he put on his business suit, grabbed his notes and went to visit with Emmanuel Macron of France. The prime minister welcomed him warmly and invited him to take a seat around the coffee table in the room.

"Mr. Macron, first of all let me congratulate you on your country's leadership on the subject of Global Warming. I am very sorry that our country pulled out of the Paris accord of 6 years ago. It was a different administration in the United States at the time, but today, I can assure you that our President, Secretary of State and the majority of U.S. citizens view climate change as a huge challenge—perhaps the biggest challenge facing our planet in the decades ahead.

"That's very good to hear. And I agree, it is a huge threat."

"So with France as a partner, I would like to take a greater leadership role in the United Nations on this subject," Graham offered.

"I think that would be very welcomed all around the globe," the Prime Minister said.

Graham agreed. "Particularly among the young people. After all, they will inherit this earth after we are long gone, and they would particularly like a clean planet. So I would like to include them more in the solution."

"It's the same in France. The young folks are the most concerned." The Prime Minister agreed.

"That's great. I am sure you know all the facts and fears about climate change. I simply want to give a progress report since you called 196 countries together six years ago. And I want to specifically enlist the young folks who may be able to make a difference in every country. Along the way, I will of course compliment France for continuing leadership on the subject, and vow to work closely with Paris in the years ahead…provided of course, that you agree."

"I not only agree. If you do address the general assembly, I will come out the next day with full support of your plan," Macron promised. "Do you still plan to meet with Ms. Tubiana? She's the one who spearheaded our efforts on this important topic."

"I do," Graham answered. "I'm having a cocktail with her tonight."

"Please say hi to her for me. She did a great job organizing the Paris conference."

"I certainly will."

The two men shook hands, and Graham was encouraged about the prospect of relighting the candle on global warming.

At the hotel, he went to the bar at 7:00 p.m., as he had promised Ms. Tubiana. He would be wearing a red tie, so she could recognize him.

Almost immediately, the woman tapped him on the shoulder and greeted him. "It's nice to meet you Mr. Kruse. I'm glad someone else can now carry to torch for climate change at the U.N."

The two talked, and Graham discovered that most of the nations had made various pledges for the cause. "Did you ever find out if they followed through?" he wondered out loud.

"Many of them did. Not all…but many. Of course, by now, it has been five or six years. Given the pace of the modern world, I am sure that many have moved on," she said.

"Well, I hope to remind the world once again as you did about the importance of this issue. Our future depends on it," he said.

"Absolutely," she agreed.

After that, they discussed the high points and the pitfalls that she had learned from her experience on the subject…and the possibility of any new initiative that might have occurred to her after the conference. She agreed that young people were key, but also business needed to play a bigger role. "It can't just be governments, it must also be in people's economic interest," she stated.

After twenty more minutes of chit-chat, Graham thanked her for all she had done and for meeting with him. She smiled and sincerely wished him good luck.

After he walked her out of the hotel, and helped her in a taxi for her ride home, Graham returned to the bar for a nightcap.

He reached for his white wine and took a sip. Before long, he noticed a very attractive woman in her early thirties who had just entered the bar. As luck would have it, she choose to sit just one stool away from him to his left.

Instinctively, he smiled at her and raised his glass as if to toast her. "Bonjour," he said. He had taken a few years of French in high school and college, but had forgotten most of it. Even so, he remembered a few words and phrases.

"Bonjour," she returned the salutation.

"Tu est Parisian?" he asked.

"No, Lyon. Est vous?

"Non, j'habite dans Les Etas Unis. Quel est votre nom?"

"Michelle," the woman answered. "Est vous?"

"Graham."

"Your French is not to bad." she remarked with a smile.

"I only know a little," he blushed.

"I only know a little English," she answered, "but luckily, we can communicate."

Graham learned that she was staying at the hotel…alone. "Do you have plans for the evening?" he asked and moved to the stool next to her. He then touched her hand sensually and smiled. "Would you like to join me in my room for a nightcap?"

She looked around the lounge to see if she recognized anyone. From the expression on her face, she did not. She then turned back to Graham, and answered, "Oui."

"That French I know….and like," Graham said and then escorted her to the elevator.

He hit 3, walked her into his room and gave her a sweet kiss on the lips.

She then unloosed his tie. He unbuttoned her blouse. Within a few minutes, they had both undressed and were hugging in bed.

Given a language barrier, it was a rather silent intercourse. However, it was a sensual experience. No rough sex, just hugs and beautiful love-making.

After a while, she picked up her watch from the end table and looked at the time. "I should go?" she gently announced.

"O.K. Michelle," Graham answered and gave her another sweet kiss on the lips as he escorted her to the door after she had dressed again. Once she had gone, he took a deep breath and smiled.

Wow, a truly sensual, harmless intercourse," he told himself. Perhaps it's a French thing. More likely, a Michelle thing, he decided.

He never learned her last name…nor her, his. As he had anticipated, he was going to thoroughly enjoy the anonymity of these assignations. If he was careful, he would most likely never get caught, and thoroughly enjoy the side benefits of international travel.

40

The General Assembly

Six weeks later, Graham has his first address at the United Nations General Assembly. The title of his speech was "One world, Geared for the Future." The subject of course was climate change.

At the risk of bragging, Graham did advance these raves to both the President and the Secretary of State.

"Bravo." was President Garvey's email. Keep up the good work."

* * * *

After a few months of positive publicity, Graham decided to embark on Mission #2. Instinctively, he knew that this subject would be more challenging. He

Once at the podium, he began his address humbly. "First of all, I would like to thank France for its leadership on this topic. I would also like to apologize for the United States backing out of the Paris accord. I intend to make amends, on behalf of the U.S. and this changing planet.

"Despite some excellent progress in the past 5-6 years, we still have a ton of work ahead of us. To this day, it remains the biggest global health threat on the planet earth. Since the beginning of this century, our dear earth is hotter than in any other decade in the past 1300 years. The temperature in the Antarctic is rising twice as fast as elsewhere on earth…and the ice is melting. Greenland is losing 279 million tons of ice a year. Global sea levels are up. It is estimated that global warming is responsible for 7 million premature deaths a year.

"So we need to act. We need to lower the CO2 emissions throughout the world. As of last year, it was the highest level in human history. We must commit to a decarbonized society. We need to quit cutting down on destroying our tropical forests. Why? 11% of all global greenhouse gasses are caused by deforestation.

"Now, how do we go about this?

"1. For one thing, we need to rely more on solar and wind energy than fossil fuels. I have spoken to my President of the United States, and he, for one, has committed to encouraging and incentivize municipalities and businesses to make that change. He is aiming for a 10% change in the next 3 years. I would like to suggest that you may be able to get the same commitment from your prime ministers or presidents.

"2. Our goal is to reduce emissions by 26%. In the U.S., we are dedicated to building more electric cars. Inevitably, that will not be the solution in every country.

But there are ways to reduce emissions, so there is less smog and dirt in the air. Let's make this a very achievable goal. Let's aim for 10% reduction in the next 3 years.

"3. This is a priority for me. Educate, convince and leverage the youth about the dangers of climate change. Fact is, many of them already recognize it as a huge problem. They think the grown-up folks like us are just viewing it an intellectual problem. They see it as a life and death danger in their lifetimes. They already believe it… but we could use even more of them to feel passionately about it, and even talk to their parents about it.

"I want to propose more involvement on their parts. Here's how: include climate change in the curriculum of colleges and universities. I am proposing a 15% increase in such classes and courses in the next three years. Try to get the leader of your nation to make that commitment. I honestly think it is achievable and will make a huge difference in the world—not just for us, but for our children and grandchildren.

"So those are three objectives. Not totally easy, but not insurmountable. Let's begin building a better environment for all the citizens of the globe. I ask all of you representatives sitting now in the United Nations, if we are not going to do it, who will? Let's start today. Thank you very much."

There was lots of applause.

Afterwards. Graham mingled with many of the representatives—all of whom congratulating him for persuading the United States to rejoin the Paris accord, and even upping the ante.

41

Follow through

As the Secretary General of the United Nations had promised, he circulated Graham's three proposals to all member representatives. By and large, he received compliments, particularly for decided to encourage the U.S. to participate in the climate change agenda. Mostly, it was the same percentage of participants as in the Paris accord. However, it did function as a way to reunite interest in global warming. Most of them signed pledges to enlist their country in this effort.

The biggest point of difference was the feedback he received in enlisting young people on this guest.

"It's ingenious," one member acknowledged.

"'I totally believe they will take it more seriously than their parents did," another answered.

"I know a bunch of young people in my country, and they are all concerned. It's a priority for them," the representative from Brazil stated.

"Hooray for the U.S. for joining the rest of the world on this mission, and for hiring a brilliant advocate," the Canadian representive gushed.

also knew from the Secretary of State that it would be more vital to the security of the United States.

It involved the proliferation of nuclear weapons in the world, particularly from North Korea.

The United Nations had a history on this subject. It was formed shortly after WWII as a safeguard for world peace. Hey, could you pick a more difficult topic?

Frankly, its success in this regard had been, at best, uneven. At last count, 31 nations in the world had ballistic missiles. Only nine—China, France, India, Israel, North Korea, Pakistan, Russia, the U.K. and the U.S—are suspected of having nuclear weapons.

As the United Nations had learned through the decades, it was a long and bumpy road to a nuclear free world. One big breakthrough was the START treaty with Russia a few decades ago, where Russia agreed to reduce weaponry. No other nation had agreed to do the same thing since. If anything, they have only increased their rocketry.

Just to illustrate the problem, the United Nations has found it difficult since its early day to negotiate schemes and bring differing parties together. All the aggressive countries believe it is in their interest to "protect themselves" and resist compromise.

In preparation for his strategy at the U.N., Graham did schedule a private meeting with the Secretary of State in Washington.

"If you can even begin to reduce tensions in this regard, you are a genius," he acknowledged. "It will be tricky. Russia and China are threats in this regard, but if you single them out, it could be the beginning of World War III."

"I agree," Graham acknowledged the risk.

"On the other hand, North Korea is our biggest threat. They are crazy, and they view as the arch enemy."

"Again, I agree." Graham said. "I would like to visit Japan again and meet with the prime minister to enlist their approval and encouragement to reduce tensions with their nasty neighbor."

"Good idea," Secretary of State Davis remarked. "And good luck."

Graham then entered into the policy arena. "By the way, here is a sensitive, and I am sure unsettled question for you. If I could suggest that the U.S, would reduce its stockpile of nuclear weapons by 10% In the next five years, would you be willing?"

Almost before he could complete his sentence, the Secretary of State interrupted him. "Of course. We have more weaponry than anyone and almost half of our missiles are getting rusty. If it will show 'good faith' on our part, I am totally in favor…especially if North Korea could agree."

"I'll give it a shot. Thank you."

In the following month, Graham asked his secretary to try to get Prime Minister Yoshida Suga of Japan on the phone. As he explained, he had met the man in New York and it would probably not be a call for him totally out of the blue.

When the telephone call went trough, he explained to an interpreter that he would like to meet again with Mr. Suga to discuss the unraveling situation between the U.S. and North Korea.

The two parties compared schedules and agreed upon a meeting on October 30 in Tokyo.

42

Arigato

On that appointed Wednesday, Graham went to the office of the prime minister of Japan and introduced himself to the secretary. She respectfully bowed and escorted him to the Prime Minister's office.

Graham thanked his for the meeting and shook hands with the translator, who he recognized from their prior get-together. He said, "the Prime Minister is very pleased to see you again…and wonders what we can do for you."

The former mayor of New York City explained his new role as the chief U.S. representative at the United Nations.

"Excellent. Congratulations," the prime minister complimented him.

After a pause, Graham finally said, "I would like to return the United Nations to its original mission after World War II. I would like to keep the world a better place in terms of world peace, harmony and human optimism. To do so, we need to reduce the military aggression from other countries, including your troublesome neighbor, North Korea.

"Good for you," Sugo said. "What do you suggest?"

"I plan to recommend a 10% reduction in all nuclear weaponry. In speaking with President Garvey and Secretary of State Davis, the U.S. will agree to this reduction, provided other nations do as well."

"Well, that's promising," the prime minister smiled. "How many other nations would that include?"

Without hesitation, Graham answered the question, "There are now 32 counties in the world that have ballistic missiles. Way too many. Perhaps we can reduce that number, thanks to the United Nations and your help."

"Let's try," the prime minister of Japan agreed with him.

"All I ask of you is this: I will stand inside the U.N. general assembly and name the countries that need to behave. Obviously, North Korea will be one of them. I simply ask you support me on this measure…for the safety of your own people and your allies around you."

"You can count on it," the Prime Minister said.

Within five minutes, there were handshakes and bows all around. Soon, Graham excused himself and caught a cab back to the Peninsula Tokyo."

* * * *

That night, Graham again went to the cocktail lounge to celebrate his latest success as U. N. ambassador.

As he had done a month ago in Paris, he ordered a white wine and sat at a stool near the bar. He then looked around the cocktail lounge to see if he might get lucky again.

Unfortunately, on this particular night, the tables were largely filled with Japanese men, all speaking in their native tongue. There were a few attractive women, but they were all with men.

Graham had a second glass and stalled for about 20 more minutes. As he reminded himself, he could always get a prostitute. However, that had never been his inclination, even as a young, sexually active single man. No, he always preferred a woman he knew by a first name. He also reminded himself that the extracurricular international sex was simply a bonus. A very nice, fun bonus...but a bonus all the same.

After his glass of wine, he proceeded to his room, and watched the international news. Unlike most of his nights, he had an early sleep. By the time he woke up for his flight to the U.S., he was poised to create talking points for his address to the United Nations on international war threats and ballistic missiles.

43

Enough weaponry

Graham had struggled with this address. Despite the fact that peace had always been a priority of the U.N., it was a difficult speech from a U.S. perspective. After all, two rival mega powers—Russia and China—were awash with nuclear weapons, and would most likely not wish to relinquish them.

However, as the representative of the U.S., and the first country ever with nuclear weapons, it was a courageous position to encourage all U.N. nations to reduce their stockpile.

When he walked up the podium, he took a deep breath, and surveyed the room.

"Good morning ladies and gentlemen. I wish you peace and prosperity in safety. It's not so easy, in this crazy world, but we in the U.N.—and perhaps only we in the U.N. --can make it a safer world.

"Perhaps it is time to be explicit," he continued. "At this exact moment, more than thirty countries currently have ballistic missiles.

"Nine of these countries have nuclear weapon. They are:

1. China
2. France
3. India
4. Israel
5. North Korea
6. Pakistan.
7. Russia
8. The U. K.
9. The U. S.

"In addition to these nuclear nations, ballistic missiles not only abound…but more and more nations are tempted to go ballistic. On behalf of the United States, we believe that is too much weaponry. It encourages aggression between nations. It makes for a more dangerous world for all citizens on the planet earth.

"So I would like to make a proposal to the countries of the United Nations.

I would like to propose reducing this weaponry. Of primary importance in this regard, I recommend no further spread of weapons between nations. It's called "horizontal proliferation." I suggest as a body, we outlaw this."

Also, I believe we must actually reduce our armaments. In discussing this with the President of the United States, we have decided to reduce our military missiles by 10% in the next three years."

There was a murmur of approval in the great hall. Graham seized on the positive reaction. "I encourage all nations to do the same," he said. "Let's make this a safer world. Will you agree to do this? Please say yes. Your citizens will thank you and so will your neighboring nations."

There was a rowdy round of applause.

It was a difficult subject to address, but Graham was glad he did so, and anxiously awaiting the results.

* * * *

Ultimately, all nations agreed to the proposal with only one exception. Guess which one? North Korea.

44

Missing the kids

It was his weekend with Michael and Rose Marie... and dad had a jam-packed agenda.

On Saturday morning, he had tickets for "The Ride." It's basically a bus ride throughout NYC, but with several different twists. For starters, the seats were arranged like theatre seats, so the patrons could get a good view of the attractions.

Along the way, Graham and the kids could witness dancers, jugglers, magicians, singers, and other street performers. The kids loved it!

After that, they went to NYC Fire Museum on Spring Street, where they saw horse drawn vehicles from the 1800's and later.

In the afternoon, they walked across the Brooklyn Bridge and enjoyed several food tours. To close out the day, they went to Broadway and saw, "Frozen."

A true thrill.

That night, over dinner, Rose Marie asked her dad if he liked his new job better than his last one.

"Well, honey, I do like this new job. It's an international job where I get the chance to see cities and countries in other parts of the world."

"Do they speak English?" Michael wondered.

"Not all of them. Many speak a language I don't understand. So I have to have a translator in many meetings. That's difficult."

"Is it more fun than being mayor of New York City?" Rose Marie wanted to know.

"No, not necessarily. Please understand, I loved being mayor of New York. But after eight years on the job, I had to do something else, at least for a little while. It's the law. However, at a certain time, I could run again for mayor. Time will tell."

Graham was please that his kids had an interest. Now it was his time to return the favor. "What about you kids? Do you like school?"

"I do," Rose Marie quickly answered.

"It's O.K.," Michael dodged.

"Do you do well? I see your report cards, and your grades look good."

It was a great give-and-take conversation. In addition to a great meal, and plenty of good sights. It was fun to see the kids begin to grow up.

On Sunday, they started the day at the American Museum of Natural History. Then they all headed to the Highline on the lower West Side. It's a good walk with plenty of places to stop for pictures and food. After lunch, they visited Madam Tussoud's wax museum. Here, he kids enjoyed images of the Wizard of Oz and ET.

They also saw life-sized figures of the Hulk and his cohorts. Afterwards, they visited the 4D theatre for an awesome Marvel comic book show.

Graham did love these weekends with his kids. Normally, he was tickled to see the kids giggle at the sights. But he also enjoyed viewing New York City through the eyes of a kid. It opened his mind as to how attractive this city was for citizens of all ages.

Of course, he could visit these sites on his own, but he had discovered it was far more fun to see them with his kids.

45

Gender Equality

His next big agenda at the United Nations was gender equality. He hoped to spearhead this initiative…but as a realist, he also recognized that it would be difficult to do so as a man alone.

In the past few years, he had become friends with many women ambassadors. He particularly enjoyed his conversations with Fatima Dias, the representative from Brazil. She was bright. She had a sense of humor, and she didn't take the job too, too seriously.

At one point, he approached her, and asked if she would like to work with him on this agenda.

"Yes, yes, yes." she responded. "That's a dynamite initiative." Then she continued. "I have seen how your work, and how you think. Smart. It tends to engage many member nations. If I can help, I would like to."

Make no mistake, despite her beautiful looks, Graham was not interested in having sex with her. Ever since he had joined the United Nations, he vowed to himself that he would not mess around with delegates who could incriminate him. On the other hand…he had heard that Brazil had many gorgeous women.

"Might we be able to get together later this winter?" she asked.

"I am free from October on," he said.

"From mid-October, I have planned to take a hiatus from the General Council.

I have already given notice to the Secretary General, and he has approved. I will be in Rio for a few months. It's a beautiful place. If you care to visit me down there, we can carve out a day to speak about this priority."

They exchanged phone numbers, and Graham agreed to call her in the early New York autumn.

On October 15, he arrived in Rio and met with Fatima. At the time, he outlined his objectives.

1. Equal pay (or at least, relative equal pay)
2. Health care for single women.
3. Women's acceptance rate in colleges and universities.

He proposed sharing the presentation load, and asked Fatima to concentrate on the global topic of equal pay. He promised to focus on health care issues, and they could share women's acceptance rates at colleges.

* * * *

In Rio, he was honestly awe struck by the beauty of this exotic city, and the women. Just to make it all the more tempting, he heard that there was nude beach only one hour from his hotel in Ipanema. It was called Abrico Beach. Having never been to such an attraction, he thought it might be a growth experience.

He decided to make the trek via Uber. He stashed some cash in his shorts, and decided, for safety sake, to keep his wallet in his hotel room.

The beach was beautiful, the sky was clear, and the temperature was warm enough for a good swim. However, Graham did not anticipate a long swim. He had another kind of exercise in mind.

As he entered the beach, he disrobed next to a woman called Regina. He introduced himself, and the two of them walked towards the water. She was completely tanned, and was evidently a regular.

After a few back and forth splashes, she put her arms around his back. He returned the favor, and before long, they were in each other's embrace. Not surprisingly, one thing led to another. She was soft and smooth, and before long he had an erection. However, he did not wish to rush things. It just felt too good feeling the current and her hands on his body.

About 15 minutes later, they climaxed. She was first, but he was less than a minute behind. Afterwards, they just hugged for another 10 minutes underwater. It felt very sexy and very, very good.

Finally, the couple exited the water together. She gave him a goodbye kiss on the lips, as did he. After dressing, he took another prearranged Uber back to his Ipanema hotel.

After a bite, he called his U.N. cohort again and reiterated how much he looked forward to their joint presentation on gender equality.

Given his earlier mutual climax with a beautiful woman named Regina, he thought of perhaps included that in the speech. He smiled at his private joke and decided it would be best to stick to his three pre-ordained objectives.

46

A call from Liz

Once back at the U.S., he decided to gather his thoughts on his latest "gender equality" topic. He started writing his parts of the presentation and had some free advice for Fatima's address. In fact, he called her in Rio, and apologized for interrupting her vacation. She urged him not to worry, and actually appreciated his thoughts.

Consequently, he continued making notes, until he got a call from Liz Quinlan, his valuable p.r. pro during his time as mayor.

She wanted to get together with him for a dinner.

"Sure," he immediately agreed. "Anything particular on your mind?"

"Lots," she replied, 'but I will explain over bread and butter."

"Can't wait," he answered. Truth is, he always had a soft spot in his heart for Liz. Yeah, she was beautiful, bearing a slight resemblance to Jennifer Lawrence.

But she was also smart. During their two terms in the mayor's office, she had protected his image frequently and often advocated his policies with the press.

Could she possibly be making a play for him? Graham privately shook his head no.

No, she was too straight arrow for that.

When she entered the restaurant, Graham gave her his usual hug and kiss on the cheek. He pulled out a chair for her. After a sweet smile, she took a deep breath. "Allow me to get the point. Penny Herzog is a disaster as mayor of New York city. For one thing, she doesn't know how to speak or deal with the press. Bear in mind, I am now out of government and back again in strait-ahead public relations…although I do miss the rough-and-tumble world of New York politics. Do you?"

"Sometimes, yes," he said

"I am a died-in-the-wool Democrat," she admitted. But at this rate, we will not win re-election. A Republican will be in charge of New York. Good news for bank C.E.Os.', and Wall Street. Bad news for the common folk who largely represent the fabric of New York City."

"So what do you suggest?" he asked.

"I want you to run for mayor again. I have researched this. After two terms, one needs to take a four-year hiatus…but then he or she can come back again and run. You should. You are well-suited for the job. And this city needs you."

"Think so?" he asked, fishing for a compliment.

"As a patriot, I think you truly must."

"If I were to run for mayor again, would you be my p.r. maven?"

She paused for a second or two, but then immediately smiled again. "It would be my honor."

* * * *

The couple concluded the evening with small talk about their latest endeavors. Since their stories did not intersect, it was a little unconnected on both their parts.

"Will you at least consider another run for mayor?" she finally broke the impasse.

"I will," he answered.

"I know them all--the players who have expressed an interest in the job. They will not win. Only you can win," she said and then reached across the table to take his hand and offer a kiss on the back of his hand. It was a reminder of the photo that immediately got him in trouble in his first term with Liz.

"Are you sure there are no cell phone photos of that touch."

"Frankly, I don't really care." She said.

"And neither do I," Graham agreed.

47

Next steps

After his and Fatima's addresses at the United Nations, many representatives congratulated both presenters. "Provocative thoughts," was one response. "Enlighted," was another. "It's about time for us to be truly egalitarian," another chimed in.

Despite the kudos, Graham began to dream of new priorities. On his agenda, he had thought of another major initiative at the U.N. It had to do with international hunger.

However, Liz had peeked his interest about the future of New York City.

In consideration of this, he called his best friend Andrew Madden. "Andy," he said, "this is your long lost friend, Graham Kruse."

"Wow, I read great things about you in your stint at the U.N. You are representing America quite well…and building a better world. Congratulations," he gushed. "How goes it?"

"It's good," he acknowledged. "And how is the job since you have returned as prosecuting attorney?"

"I have enjoyed it…and my wife is happy to see me at home at the end of the day. What's on your mind?"

Graham paused and then spoke, "I got an unusual call from Liz and had dinner with her."

"You didn't do anything nasty with her this time, did you?"

"Not yet." Graham chuckled.

"However, her lament was about the current state of New York City. According to her, Mayor Herzog is an absolute waste.

"Well, she is 100% correct in her assessment," Andy quickly agreed. "At this rate, she will be easily defeated by any Republican in the contest. What does she suggest?"

"She wants me to run for mayor again," he answered.

"Can you?"

"Actually, I could. After two terms, one must take four years off…but then if one so chooses, he or she can run again."

"Are you so inclined?" Andy sincerely asked.

"I'm not quite sure yet," Graham answered. "But I miss the progress we made in New York."

"As do I," Andy answered. "However, I am committed to my job at prosecuting attorney. I promised my wife I would be there for the years ahead."

"I understand," Graham responded. "I'm not sure I will even run. But if it do, I will let you know."

"Please do…and as Liz suggested, it would be a good thing for the citizens of New York City," Andy said. He then said, "Good luck," and hung up.

48

Adios U. N.

Four months later, Graham called President Garvey and the Secretary of State to give them fair warning that he was considering another run as mayor of New York City. Obviously, it would mean the end of his tenure as the ambassador at the United Nations.

"No," President Garvey objected. "You have been an amazing ambassador. The whole world loves you and respects you, as so I"

"I appreciate that," Graham said. "However, my kids are in New York, and I wish to visit them more frequently. Also, I tend to have a life-long attraction to this great city. And I am told that if I don't run, this great place could fall into Republican hands.

"Not likely," the President asserted.

"Well, you never know," Graham opined.

The President spoke persuasively for the next twenty minutes about the job the former mayor had done at the United Nations.

Ten minutes later, Secretary of State Davis called Graham and tried to convince him to stay in the job. "We are a damn good team… and the best is yet to come. Think of all the progress we can make on behalf of the United States."

"I have. But I also want to make progress for New York City. As I told the President, it's home for me and my kids."

* * * *

There were five Democratic candidates who had announced their intention to run for mayor of New York. Three of them were deputy mayors, who Graham knew well. As he privately admitted to himself, they were losers.

The other two were borough leaders. However, as most people already knew, they were weak candidates.

The President himself leaked to the two New York Senators that it was likely that Graham Kruse would run again for mayor.

"Wow," Senator Donahue exclaimed. "It sounded like he was doing an amazing job at the U.N."

"He was," the President agreed. "However, I think he wants to spend a little more time with his kids, and he misses the Big Apple."

Senator Johnson was equally dumbfounded. "Damn," the Senator from Kingston, New York said. "However, it sounds like New York City could use his steady hand again."

Within a matter of days, all the New York City newspapers covered the scoop.

"Kruse wants to be back in saddle again," the *New York Post* declared. "Welcome again," the *Daily News* declared. The *New York Times* printed an article that covered three columns. It was titled, "What Kruse means to this city." It basically chronicled his accomplishments as mayor, and anticipated further achievements if he were elected again.

That night, Graham made another call to Liz Quinlan, his favorite public relations person. "I hear my message must have gotten through to you," she said.

"See, I listen to you," Graham said.

"When will you officially announce?"

"I will need to come up with objectives and priorities. Maybe you can help me brainstorm one night."

"I would be glad to," Liz answered. "Will Andy serve again as your right hand man?"

"I don't think so. I spoke with him, and he wants to continue to serve as prosecuting attorney. He likes the job. He knows the job. Also, he wants to spend more time with his family."

"Wow, that's too bad," she remarked. You two got along so great."

"True, but I hope you will join me in this endeavor. You know I trust your judgment."

"You can count on me," she said.

"I do, and I will," Graham answered. "I'll give you a call in a few weeks so we can brainstorm some meaningful objectives for the next four years."

"Sounds good," Liz answered, and genuinely looked forward to that get-together.

49

Rose Marie, Michael and dad

It was Graham's weekend with the kids, and on this glorious summer weekend, it was a great time to sightsee the city.

He decided to start out with a bike ride. Citi rents those blue bikes and includes free helmets, locks and maps. In addition there is a bike path all along the Hudson River, and the kids were now of an age (10 and 8) that they could negotiate the path with safety. Graham trailed behind and kept a watchful eye on Rose Marie and Michael. The family got a good hour of exercise, and even stopped for soft drink half way through the journey.

After this, Graham called his driver to meet him on 63rd and schedule a few fun activities. For starters, they went to Central Park and enjoyed a boat ride on that big lake in the center of the park. Graham did most of the rowing, and the kids enjoyed the scenery.

Then they all went to the New York Botanical Garden and viewed acres of plant life. Given the time of the year, many of the trees and plants were in full bloom. For dinner, they shared burgers and fries at the Shake Shack.

The next day, Graham treated them all to the Statue of Liberty and Ellis Queens. Here, they saw many exhibits and got choice seats for one of the best kid movies ever filmed. It was "2001: A Space Odyssey." Island. Lots of pictures of the kids together and with their dad. They did get a guided tour, so they all learned the history of the monument and heard about the millions of people who came to New York City via Ellis Island. In all, more than twelve million immigrants entered the United States from this small island. "That's more people than live in the city right now," Dad explained.

In the afternoon, they visited the Museum of the Moving Image in Astoria. In the main theatre there, they were showing "Superman." Both Rose Marie and Michael loved it, as did Graham who hadn't seen the film in decades.

The family closed out the Sunday with dinner at Café Luxembourg. It had always been one of Graham's favorite places, and they had plenty of things the young people could like.

During dinner, Michael asked his dad if knew that mom seemed to now have a boyfriend. "Is that true, Rose Marie?"

"Yep,"the young girl answered. "Did she not tell you?"

"No," dad replied. "But she doesn't have it. She has her own life." After a bite, he asked his son, "What's the guy's name?"

"Brad."

"What's he do?" Graham asked his daughter.

"I think he teaches at that school where mom worked…or maybe he's the new principal."

"Well, that's good, I guess," their dad stated. "At least they have some things in common."

"Guess so," Michael answered.

Graham was tempted to ask if they kids liked him. However, he decided that could very well be Pandora's Box. And it might open a bunch of questions about his interest in women. No, better to let it be."

As promised, he returned the kids to their Upper West Side apartment. He watched them scamper to the front door, waved goodbye and sent a kiss through the air.

Before he asked his driver to leave, he paused and took another look at the residence. Prior to the divorce, it had been the source of many happy times. Still, he had happy times with the kids…albeit on a monthly basis.

Quite frankly, Graham was surprised that Linda had moved closer to happiness with a new fellow. He did not begrudge her this. Truth be told, he was semi-surprised it had taken her so long.

In a perverse way, he believed it sort of freed him --not that he needed much more freedom to entertain and be entertained by other women. However, perhaps it could liberate him to have a more serious relationship.

"Who knows?" he thought. Maybe what's good for the gander may also be good for the goose.

50

New objectives for a new term

By mid-week, he had booked a table for two at Tocqueville Restaurant on West 15th Street. It's a French restaurant with excellent food and uncrowded tables, so Liz and Graham could have a good talk without eavesdroppers.

"Have you been here before," Graham asked.

"Nope, it's a first…but I hear it's good" she answered.

"It's great," he said, and ordered a few cocktails.

"Have you been thinking of priorities for my next term, assuming I will be elected," Graham asked.

"A few. Strange to think of this in such an elegant restaurant, but what about hunger in New York City."

"Hard to think of that right now," he smiled.

"I know."

"I was wondering about affordable housing," he said. "People are evicted every day in this city. I think it's awful…especially if it's a family with several kids, and maybe a grandmother"

"Where do they go?" she wondered.

"A lot of them have to leave the city, or even the state," Graham believed.

"I think it's cheaper down South in Mississippi or Alabama. I'll bet it's cheaper in the Dakotas too."

"Yeah, but then they have to leave all their friends here in New York City."

"I want to preserve or build at least 100,000 affordable units in the next 4 years. Or at least give tax breaks to the landlord's who want to participate. It should cost one-third or less of a household's income…and the rent cannot increase drastically over time. With the Department of House Preservation and Development, it could also be good for seniors."

"That sounds good," Liz silently clapped encouraged him. "Got another bright idea?"

"This one I love," he nodded. "I have noticed more and more traffic jams in the city."

"That's for sure," she agreed.

"Too many cars, especially at rush hour. Too many people driving all alone inside a vehicle."

"And the solution is……"

"Everybody uses EZ pass to go over the bridges these days. I think if we were to include a video camera that would capture whether the cars have more than one person in them. If they do, they should get a cheaper fare to enter the city. It could reduce traffic jams by 50%."

"I think that's brilliant," Liz acknowledged.

"You really like it?"

"I love it!"

"So that's two. That should hold me over for a few years, provided I can get elected again."

"You'll get elected. I'll make sure of it"

"Promise?"

"Promise.

He then passed a menu to her. "Come on, let's order." He wanted scallops, she preferred the crab cakes. Meanwhile, they discussed the contours of the upcoming election.

"So you're going to get me elected," he teased her.

"I did last time, didn't I?"

"You certainly did."

"I think you should make your announcement in Times Square, right by that George M.Cohan's statue."

"Why there?"

"Because you love the arts and you love music."

"That is true," he said.

"Incidentally, Penny Herzog has just announced she is not going to run for re-election. I think that when she heard you were jumping back in the race, it was curtains for her."

"Maybe so." He shrugged.

"If I make the announcement in Times Square, will you make sure there are plenty of press people there?"

"Of course." she responded and ordered come coffee as the denouement of the meal. Once they had each finished, he picked up the tab and walked her to a cab. As he was prone to do with her, he gave her a big hug and kiss on the cheek.

* * * *

Two weeks later, Graham made his announcement in Times Square. Not surprisingly, there were plenty of reporters on hand to cover the event. Most of them raved about the job he had done, and predicted that he would most likely win again. As the former mayor told himself, "It's too early to get cocky. He did gleefully accept the applause, and reminded himself that "Only time will tell."

51

I Missed You, NYC

While he still had some loose ends to tie up as ambassador of the United Nations, Graham thought it was only right to vacate his penthouse apartment near the headquarters. After all, he had already resigned to the President and the Secretary of State. Also, he had announced his candidacy for mayor. Besides, it might be fun to explore another part of the city.

He looked in the *Village Voice* to find apartment sublets. Here, he found the name of Beth Harrison, who wrote in a classified ad that she was the expert in finding the right sublet for the right person.

A sublet was all he wanted. He had some confidence he would be re-elected mayor of New York City. Of course, it wasn't a sure thing. But if he did win again, he would need a place until Gracie Mansion opened up for him.

When he reached Beth on the telephone, he told her he would probably be most interested in Greenwich Village, Chelsea, or maybe Murray Hill.

"Let's start looking in Murray Hill," she suggested. "I just have a few in that neighborhood, but I have loads available in the village and in Chelsea."

When he arrived at their meeting point at 160 East 38th and Third Avenue, he was struck by the beauty of his real estate agent. She looked as exotic as Mila Kunis. In addition, she was amazingly friendly and outgoing, "Wow, I get to spend most of the day with the once and future mayor," she remarked and gave him a hug and kiss.

"Well, well, well…someone as affectionate as I have always been," he said to himself.

The apartment itself was quite beautiful. It was a townhouse on a private street. It contained three bedrooms and was beautifully decorated.

"Wanna see more," Beth asked.

"I want to see all three neighborhoods," he answered.

The next apartment was on 39th and Park Avenue. It was a high-rise. Very convenient to Grand Central, but he didn't particularly like the traffic that would inevitable be going to and from the train station.

Next stop: Chelsea. Graham always rather enjoyed Chelsea. He liked Chelsea Pier where you can drive golf balls and Chelsea Market, one of the best grocery shops in the city. In addition, he got a kick for the Highline, where he walked and talked with Beth at least for 20 minutes. She was pleasant company on this beautiful, sunny afternoon. Together, they looked at five sublets from West 43rd down to West 19th. The prices were rather affordable—from $3000 to $5000 per month. Most of them were nicely furnished. However, Graham didn't exactly flip over any other units.

Consequently, they headed down to Greenwich Village. Here, they looked at five more apartments. As opposed to high-rise buildings in other neighborhoods, he appreciated the townhouse appeal of this area.

The one place that immediately charmed him was a place called "Alabama Living," It was built in 1903, and was very convenient on 15 East 11th. It was close to Washington Square Park and very accessible to so many subway lines. In addition, it was a full-service building with a 24-hour business center. It also had a pool and a fitness center. The 3-bedroom place was elegantly furnished and fairly affordable—a sublet of only $4500 per month.

"Wow," Graham reacted as he walked through all the rooms and then onto the balcony.

"You like it?" she asked and could predict the answer.

"It's perfect!"

Beth joined him on the balcony, and said, "Let's get it!" She then put her arm around Graham and gave him a kiss on the lips. She then walked him back to the master bedroom and sat on the King bed.

"You think it fits my personality?" he asked.

She then stood up and faced him. Without hesitation, she put both hands on his ass and rubbed a bit. "Let's try it out. Maybe we should inaugurate this bed and see how well it works."

To be perfectly honest, Graham was befuddled with her advances. Once upon a time, he was used to such flirtations from an attractive woman. But it had been awhile. Lately, he had done most of the seductions.

He walked away from her and shook his head trying to clear his mind. Something told him this was wrong….something, or someone.

Instead, he told Beth that he was indeed interested in the apartment and would send her a check tomorrow. It was the last time he would speak with her, and the last time he would stand next to a bed with her.

52

A big day in the campaign

June 15th and June 16th were important days for Graham Kruse. As he told Liz Quinlan, he anticipated good news on three fronts:

First of all, he received a call from President Garvey last week asking if it would help the campaign if he visited next week and campaigned with the mayoral prospect.

"Are you kidding? It would be a godsend." Graham reacted.

"I would suggest we do it outside the U.N. headquarters, the President offered. That way, I can brag about the job you did for the U.S. government, and wish you well in your upcoming race."

"Let's make it around 1 p.m. I will alert the press," the candidate promised.

"And the 16th is a big day for you too." Liz teased.

"That's the Democratic primary, my dear."

"Oh, I almost forgot, she chuckled. "Actually, I already booked Rockefeller Center for that night."

"You are a true pro," he said with admiration.

"And you said, you anticipated good news on three fronts," she remembered.

Graham grinned at his private secret. At the podium, there were American flags to the right and left, and Graham did recognize some of the representatives to the U.N. who had come to know over the past few years. Finally, Liz asked the unanswered question. "What's the third thing?"

"I get to spend two full days with you."

"Wow, you are smooth," she commented.

* * * *

When the President came to town, Graham met up with him an hour beforehand.

Inevitably, the two men compared notes about their activities over the past several weeks. After a short while, it was time for the men to speak.

The President began his address by welcoming the crowd and the press who had turned out. "I'm glad you all did because I wanted to underscore what an asset Graham Kruse was when working for the White House."

"He made persuasive arguments on behalf of America for climate change, the reduction of ballistic missiles, and gender equality. The man is thinking all the time, and seems to have a gift for persuading people around him that there is a better path, a more enlightened approach, and a smarter outcome if we all put our heads together.

"I know he did that when he was mayor of New York City, and I am fully confident that he will do that again in the months ahead. We will miss him, but he told me that in heart, he believed he belonged here.

"So good luck, my dear friend. As the saying goes, our loss is your gain."

There was a hearty round of applause. In a few minutes, Graham took the podium and addressed his admirers. "It was high honor to serve the President and the United States. What a country. I very much enjoyed working with the representatives to the U.N. and continue to believe that the organization is essential for world peace and a shared sense of humanity. We all need each other...and I don't just mean our neighbors. We need to appreciate and value the men and women who live on the other side of the planet, under different kinds of governments and regional pressures. As I used to remind myself in the wee hours, if we work together, we can build a better world. It's not too late. Let's start doing it today."

Again, there was another round of applause. Graham personally came up the President for handshakes and pictures. They were in all the New York newspapers the next day.

* * * *

The next day, Graham considered what he would tell his fans when he won the Democratic primary, which he fully expected.

It was a landslide. Kruse got more than 60% of the total vote. Of the other five candidates, no one exceeded 9%.

For old time's sake, the candidate invited his best friend and former deputy mayor, Andrew Madden, to the celebration. "I'm so glad you came," the candidate said, "And I am so appreciative of all you did during my first two terms."

"It was my pleasure," Andy answered. "And congratulations. It was a very big win."

Eventually, when the results were a foregone conclusion, Liz Quinlan walked up to the podium and introduced Graham to the crowd.

"Hello, friends," he began. "You all made all the difference in this race. I couldn't do it alone. But even when I was travelling out the country, I truly believed this is the best city on earth, which houses the best citizens.

"All people want here is the chance to experience the excitement that pervades New York City every single day. They want the chance to build a bright future for their kids. They want safety during the day and late at night. They want the kind of thrills you can't find in any other city. They want beauty. They want friendship. They want art, music, humor and health. And I intend to make sure that our citizens can have all that, and more.

"I thank you all for your votes and your continuing support. On to November! Let's make these next four years ones to remember. Thanks. Enjoy the rest of your evening, and the rest of the campaign."

The crowd did more than applaud. They actually cheered.

* * * *

"That was excellent, as usual," Liz told the successful candidate, and brought him a glass of white wine for a private toast.

"Thanks to you," he avowed, "Great turnout. Are up ready for my third bit of good news." he asked.

"Not yet."

"Well, I don't think I could come up with a better time than tonight."

"I almost forgot it," she winked at him.

"I get to spend the whole time with you," he reminded her. They clinked glasses and then he gave her a hug and a kiss.

"Have you seen my new apartment," he asked.

"Not yet," she answered.

"Let me be your tour guide," he teased, and opened the door to a taxi which they shared. It was not the only thing they shared that night. It was almost as if each of them expected such an outcome.

53

Running again

As he had done in the past two mayoral campaigns, the Democratic candidate spent a fair amount of time on talk shows promoting his vision for New York City.

From his last go-around, he had particularly enjoyed *The View*, especially since Whoopie Goldberg had suggested that perhaps he should for mayor the first time. Of course, times change, and the group wanted to know his big burning issues this time.

"Well, for one thing, perhaps you have heard that I want to reduce traffic jams in New York city, which is why I want people to pool together in cars, especially ones that are creating delays over every bridge and tunnel going in and out of the city. But it isn't all about traffic," Graham admitted.

"When I was working at the United Nations, I realized too many cars drastically reduce the air, pollution and emission qualities all over the world. It creates more dirt in the air, and that is bad for daily life of anyone who walks in this city. It's bad for people trying to have lunch. It's bad for kids at recess or getting out of school. It's particularly bad for seniors, and this city increasingly has an aging population.

"Really," Meghan McCain reacted skeptically. "I always think of New York as a very young city."

"Well, it's changing. Seniors in the city now constitute 13% of the population—up almost 10% in the last decade. Overall, this group of older citizens is growing faster than that of younger individuals. But the traffic congestion, particularly in the mid-town, affects everyone."

"Wow, you really do your homework. Bet you did well in school" Joy Behar quipped.

"Well, the one thing I have learned as I get older, is that need to never quit learning…especially if you hope to help people who live in this great city," the candidate admitted with some humility.

* * * *

On CNN, he had an interview with Fredricka Whitfield. She too invited him to discuss priorities that should maybe be addressed in the next four years.

"Given how long New York City has been in business, I would suggest that we need to take a good look at our bridges, roads and buildings. They are getting older, and they are consequently, less safe."

"So how do you fix that?" she asked.

"There's only one solution. It's called money, "Graham answered. "I believe we need to look at our tax rate in New York City. So many people are struggling to get by, so I am not suggesting raising their taxes. However, there are many people who financially benefit from living in the business capital of America. I believe that if we inch their taxes upward, it wouldn't damage their ability to enjoy all that this city has to offer. Also, it would benefit the infrastructure of New York City. If we don't fix it soon, it will begin to fall apart," he remarked.

On the Shephard Smith program on CNBC, Graham had an unusual suggestion. "I think the citizens of this great city need to be healthier. That probably means more exercise."

"How do we do that? Should more people walk to work?"

"If they can, yes. Perhaps at least one day a week. There are plenty of gyms and physical fitness places around town, but perhaps you have noticed, they are rather costly."

"I have noticed that," Shephard Smith agreed.

"I'll give families an idea. Just a few weeks ago, I went biking with two of my kids on that bike path along the Hudson River.

They absolutely loved it. And it was cheap. The maps, locks and the helmets are free!"

"You see these rows of bikes all over in the city. They are called Citi bikes. You know, the blue ones. I think it only costs about ten bucks to rent one for an hour. The fresh air will invigorate you, and you'll feel better after pedaling around town. If you've got kids, I'd stay off the streets. Look for those bike paths near the water. They are safer."

"I like that idea," Shephard Smith said. "Maybe I'll try it this weekend.

"Nice job," Liz acknowledged after watching the shows. "I like all three proposals, and I think New York City will love them. Maybe I could go biking with you some day," she said.

"I would absolutely love that," Graham answered, and looked forward to such an outing.

54

The General

Graham's Republican opponent, a middle-aged executive at Merrill Lynch named Arthur Garrison, had received some good publicity in the next month. He tended to get on all the business programs and advocated that New York citizens be more careful investing their money. "Don't get too risky," he would tell them. "Balance your portfolio."

The Democratic candidate wondered why he was getting airtime. Perhaps he has a message that is resonating with folks," he told Liz.

"I doubt it, "she answered. "He's just a new face."

"I think I told you that Rockefeller Center would be ideal. You should begin thinking of what to say. If you wish, I will help you."

"I'll give it a crack. Appearances on all those talk shows help prepare me for what resonates with people."

"Don't worry my friend. You are way ahead, by at least 25 points," Liz reassured him.

"You're not just saying that to make me feel good, are you?"

"No way, the circulation of your news endorsements outnumber his by 90%."

After a pause, he asked he p.r. pro if she had been thinking about the party after the General Election.

* * * *

Before long, it was Autumn in New York City. November was on its way, and that would be the general election for mayor.

Again, most of the newspapers endorsed Graham Kruse. "He seems to only get better with every new challenge," the *New York Times* reported. Even the President of the United States came to town to brag about the job Kruse had done while serving as ambassador at the U.N."

The *New York Post* boasted about his proposals. The *Daily News* claimed that he was the only one in the race that has the experience and sensitivity to help all people of New York City get ahead.

Only the *Wall Street Journal* recommended Garrison. "Isn't it time for a change of pace?" the paper asked. "Perhaps it's time for someone who knows dollars and cents as much as arts and leisure."

On the afternoon of the general election, there was an excellent, impressive turnout. It was far bigger than the amount that voted for Penny Herzog and her opponent four years ago. Actually, it was even bigger than either of Graham's two previous elections.

By ten p.m., many of the precincts had reported. The vast majority were in the Democratic column. By 10:45, Arthur Garrison conceded and congratulated Graham for running a very honorable campaign and for ultimately winning a third term.

At 11 p.m. Liz shared that news with Graham and suggested that he give his address before he started to lose the crowd. "If it's O.K with you, I will give you a short introduction. There are dozens of reporters here, so remember to wave to them, your volunteers, and all the people who came out to be with you on this winning night."

In a few minutes, Liz took the microphone and introduced the newly elected mayor of New York City. "Ladies and gentlemen, please give a warm welcome to Mayor Graham Kruse. I have known him for many years now, and I assure you couldn't have elected a better man."

Graham trotted to the podium and grabbed the mike. "I am so happy to be here again," he said. "It's a wonderful victory, thanks to all of you. I want to thank all of the newspapers, TV stations and radio stations that supported our candidacy. But most of all, I want to thank all of the people in the crowd who stood in line to vote.

"I want to assure you that this does not get old. If anything, I am more encouraged by this result than any of my other victories. I am told it is the biggest turnout in 12 years.

"As I am sure many of you know, I plan to prioritize reducing the traffic jams in New York, rebuilding the crumbling infrastructure and making this a healthier city for all of our citizens.

"I also hope to visit more of the outer boroughs this year, and make this a better environment for kids. As the father of two, I can think of no better mission...so enjoy the celebration tonight. Tomorrow, we will need to get back to work. So tonight, let's have some fun. Thank you all for turning out, and be careful on the way home."

With that, he waved to the crowd and circulated among many of the people who had turned out on his behalf. Some were news folks. Others were elected officials. The vast majority were supporters.

"You did a great job, Liz," Graham said and gave her a hug and kiss. "Do you have to get to work early tomorrow?

"Not really," she answered. "I knew it would be a late night, and I didn't schedule anything for the next day."

"You want to ride some bicycles tomorrow," he innocently asked.

"Among other fun things," she said with a wink.

After many goodbyes to his many volunteers, the newly elected mayor offered Liz a cab ride to his new apartment in the Village.

55

The Morning After and the Days Ahead

That evening, the couple had a private celebration. Despite the late hour, they still had much to discuss, much to accomplish, and much to enjoy.

Indeed, it had been a long time since Graham had first reached for her outstretched hand when he had first run for mayor. So much had happened since then—a second term, life in the United Nation as a representative of the United States, and now the election to a third term (not to mention the sexual detours all along the way).

As he stood there and looked at her longingly for the second time in a month, Graham had to wonder what took him so long. By god, she was a beautiful woman, and a very smart one who was always in his corner.

Around midnight, they went on the balcony and congratulated each other on a campaign well run. "We're a good team," the newly elected mayor said. "I knew it from the start."

"So did I," Liz agreed. "But I just didn't want either of us to get ahead of our skis."

Almost involuntarily, Graham gave her a warm embrace and looked out over the city, still ablaze in lights. She returned the hug. Nothing lewd or naughty. Just something like love.

After a few moments touching her hair, he asked her if she would consider working in the mayor's office. "I could really use someone as smart as you by my side. I honestly think I work better, more intelligently, more clearly when you are around. Also, it is just more fun. I know it would mean walking away from your public relations firm, but we could do great things together."

"I think we could," she nodded. "And I really enjoy being with you."

"Let's do it then," he smiled and walked her to the king-sized bed. The two almost mirrored each other's moves. There was a touch on both cheeks. There was a gentle back rub. There was the culmination of squeezes and cuddles. And of course, there was the happiness when both of them just giggled and looked at the ceiling.

After about another hour respite, she reached out to him for a repeat performance. Unlike other pushy, aggressive women that he had met, this was just sweet. After another half hour, the two just embraced and started to dream.

"Is this place expensive?" Liz asked.

"It's not that expensive, and the mayor's job pays well. I could maybe swing it, if you like it."

"Well, I have had fun here," she chuckled.

"As have I, with you."

"Let's keep it then." She sincerely added.

Damn, he told himself. "This is about as good as it gets."

The two of them snuggled and hugged under covers. At 7:30, they both awoke,

"I'm going to miss this place," Graham said.

"Do you have to get rid of it," she asked.

"Well, not necessarily….however, I will have Gracie Mansion, at least in a few months, but it's a little deadly on the weekends. My kids don't like to visit. I think they have only been to Gracie Mansion one weekend or two. Also, it's way uptown, in the middle of nowhere." They then showered and prepared for breakfast downstairs. It was scram eggs for each of them, along with bacon and toast. He showed her the gym, the pool, and the area on the main floor, where each could work. Both had a cup of coffee to prepare for bright, new day. They silently smiled at each other, and quietly enjoyed each other's company.

Upon finishing their coffees, the couple exited the apartment. Instinctively, The couple walked hand in hand, until they reached the citi bike display about a block away.

"Look at that bright, blue sky. It's a beautiful day for a ride," Graham suggested.

"I thought you'd never ask," Liz said. With that, both of them straddled their blue bikes and headed down the road until they hit the bike path, and then they proceeded uptown. They sincerely believed it would be a very good journey ahead.